# THE WEALTHY BARMAID

*From Minimum Wage to Millionaire*

by Melanie Bajrovic

Published by Best Seller Publishing®, Pasadena, CA

Best Seller Publishing® is a registered trademark

Printed in the United States of America.

ISBN: 978-1-946978-09-7

This publication is designed to provide accurate and authoritative information with regard to the subject matter covered. It is sold with the understanding that the publisher is not engaged in rendering legal, accounting, or other professional advice. If legal advice or other expert assistance is required, the services of a competent professional should be sought. The opinions expressed by the authors in this book are not endorsed by Best Seller Publishing® and are the sole responsibility of the author rendering the opinion.

Most Best Seller Publishing® titles are available at special quantity discounts for bulk purchases for sales promotions, premiums, fundraising, and educational use. Special versions or book excerpts can also be created to fit specific needs.

For more information, please write:

Best Seller Publishing®

1346 Walnut Street, #205

Pasadena, CA 91106

or call 1(626) 765 9750

Toll Free: 1(844) 850-3500

Visit us online at: www.BestSellerPublishing.org

# CONTENTS

# INTRODUCTION

I believe that you and I are more alike than you might think. You are the type of person who knows what they want and who knows that they are capable of achieving more. I applaud you for being part of the 1% that will actually get out there and do whatever it takes to make their dream a reality. You are one of the select few who will actually do something about your current situation.

If you are reading this book, then you are aware of your unique ability to seek betterment in all aspects of your life. You know that you can take everything to the next level. You know that you do not have to settle for anything short of a masterpiece.

I have always been an introspective, eager, and inquisitive type of person. I always try improving things in any part of my life where I feel there is discomfort. Initially, it was always about financial security for me, and over the course of my experiences it became about financial freedom, which is exactly what this book covers. Through my own experiences, I learned that three aspects of my life, working together, are what got me where I am today. The Wealthy Barmaid Formula is:

- Always Working
- Always Saving
- Always Investing

I may have started as a barmaid, but I always had a burning desire to achieve more, to do more, and to try new things. As a young girl, I was fortunate to have exposure to the business and investing strategies of my grandparents, parents, and uncle. These strategies were the building blocks that I played with from a young age. It is important to note that my success did not happen overnight. I managed to progress little by little, adding every block with purpose, and with each step taken I was building a mini-empire right before my eyes. Year after year, I continued to increase my income and my net worth.

The lessons that I learned throughout my youth are absolutely invaluable. I will be forever grateful for receiving them as they guided my path to becoming a millionaire before turning thirty. During my journey, I realized that everyone does not necessarily believe in investing, nor do they learn about it during their childhood. I also realized that the investment knowledge that I had at my fingertips, as basic information, was not commonly known to the majority of the population. I wrote this book to share my strategies with you in the hope that you will be able to clearly define and then achieve your vision of financial freedom.

# From Yugoslavia, With Love

Sixty-nine dollars. That's where my story begins. It was an investment my grandparents made in 1970. It was an investment in the future. And it was all the money they had.

My grandparents were from Serbia, then a part of the former Yugoslavia. They lived fairly well in the small town of Apatin, two and a half hours north of Belgrade. My grandfather was a salesman for a thriving sock company and my grandmother was a stay-at-home mom. They were living with their parents (my great-grandparents) and there was no mortgage on the house as the government gave all residents their homes mortgage-free after World War II. Yugoslavia was under communist rule and everybody lived decently. There were no large divisions of class and everyone had the basic necessities.

But even still, my grandfather knew that he could do much better in the capitalism of the West. Capitalism provided more opportunity and my grandfather dreamed of a more fruitful life for not only his wife and two children, but for the generations of his family to come. My Grandfather's vision was to move his family to Canada, considered the land of opportunity for many in the Eastern bloc nations of the time. His uncle, George, in fact, was already living there.

And so, in February of 1970, with only sixty-nine dollars in their pockets, my grandparents packed up and left the relative security of communist Yugoslavia for a chance at a better life. With their kids in tow, and not knowing a lick of English, they journeyed to the home of my great-uncle in Orillia, Ontario. They would stay with Uncle George for a month, to settle in and come up with a game plan to begin creating the better life they had sought.

This bold, courageous move inspires me to this day. The difficulties of being an immigrant in a brand-new country where everything is different (even the opposite) from what you have known, not knowing the language, and trying to survive while caring for a family of four, are almost unimaginable to me. But even more unimaginable, and more admirable, is the fact that my grandparents not only survived, they thrived.

In Orillia, they wasted no time in putting their kids in school to acclimate them to the society and culture at large. Their next step was to find work. A friend in Niagara told them there was a large Serbian community in that area, so they decided to look for jobs there, maybe eventually put down roots in Niagara. They had to leave the kids with Uncle George, but knew it would only be for a short time while they found jobs and a place to live.

After about a month they found work and a place to rent. As soon as they were settled, they returned to Orillia for their children, and started living life as a whole family in Niagara. My grandmother started out cleaning rooms at a local motel, and my grandfather would pick worms at night to sell to fishermen. They had tons of odd jobs along the way because they would take any opportunity available to them to earn extra money. Simultaneously, they were taking night classes to learn English, which was very difficult for them. They were over forty, and they only knew Serbian. Previously, they had never spoken another language.

My grandmother eventually got a job at a leather wallet factory, and she earned a little more money than she did at the motel. She would later transition to another factory that made tackle boxes, as well as another where she canned juices. It was all fairly laborious work, which was all they could get at the time. My poor grandmother always dealt with health issues, making her a little weak physically, but she still needed to meet her quotas. Sometimes, my mother would go in with my grandmother to help so she wouldn't get fired.

No matter how she felt physically though, my grandmother never stopped. Even to this day, at seventy-seven, you will never catch her without a broom in her hand. She comes around to my restaurant and she picks weeds or sweeps the patio. She helps me out when I renovate my investment properties. Both my mother and my grandmother are very strong-willed women. They will never be defeated, and that perseverance keeps them going. Their hard work has been a major inspiration to me since I was a little girl. I will always look up to them and admire their strength.

A little while later, my grandfather seized an opportunity to work for a wine manufacturing facility. This job paid $1.25 an hour. He told me stories about how while it was heavy labor, it paid well at the time, and he was just happy to have the work. He was able to transition to another factory at $1.75 an hour. He was slowly moving up the job ladder at the manufacturing plant but again, he was always grateful.

My grandparents lived frugally. They ate "peasant food" a lot of the time. They were living in studio or bachelor apartments with a family of four. There wasn't a lot of money to work with, but they spread it out very well. My grandfather remembers a very impactful day when my mother asked him, "Daddy, when will we have Coca-Cola in the house?" She always saw other kids at school drinking Coca-Cola, bringing cans of pop to enjoy at lunch, and longed to have some of her own. Her question absolutely killed my grandfather. From that moment and onward, he did everything in his power (as if he didn't have enough motivation already) to make sure he would someday be able to provide his children with everything they could ever want or need.

In 1972, after a couple years of conscientious effort, they managed to save $1,000 – and it was with this money that they bought their first house! Before coming to North America, my grandfather knew that the way to be truly successful here was to have your own business as well as your own real estate. Achieving both of these aspects was his goal right from the start, and after saving money from "next-to-nothing" pay, he was able to fulfill half of his plan. My grandfather then quickly learned that location matters…a lot.

Around 1974, he realized that values were not increasing in his area. However, he started noticing that houses in a nearby neighborhood were annually increasing 5% to 10% in value. So they ended up staying for one more year in their first house and managed to save another $2,500. Once they were established, they put their home up for sale, and bought another house in a better neighborhood where they lived for another two years.

They continued to work as their children went to school, all the while letting everyone acclimate to their new environment. My grandparents did their best, and they kept growing little by little. Their methods were not very attractive to most people necessarily, because they remained very frugal, saving every penny for the betterment of their future.

After being in this country for a few years, they finally decided that working for someone else and living paycheck to paycheck was not how they were going to meet their goals. After working a variety of different jobs, they decided to sell their second home in order to purchase their first piece of commercial real estate, which was a restaurant/bar including a second-floor apartment.

My grandfather recognized the real estate potential in North America, and also saw the necessity of having his own business. It was time to fulfill the other half of his plan. They combined their savings and the money from the sale of the second house and purchased their first commercial property. They lived in the apartment upstairs while they tried their hands in the bar industry; which they knew nothing about. There was a night when someone asked my grandmother for a screwdriver. She of course replied "yes," and then she went into the back and literally grabbed them a Phillips screwdriver from the toolbox!

My grandparents were completely unfamiliar with cocktails and drinks, and generally what it meant to run a business. They still were not fluent in English, but they continued doing their best. They found their solutions as they moved forward. Day after day, night after night, they were dedicated, and they would try everything they could to get things done properly. Because things were not very successful in the beginning, my grandfather returned to welding in order to make ends meet. My grandmother focused on running the bar as well as learning the industry itself.

When business started to pick up ten months later, my grandfather was able to quit his welding job. He was so happy to finally work with my grandmother at the bar full time. My grandparents would have lived frugally for as long as it took, saving their money and looking for new ways to invest. However, they were finally able to begin cracking the code to building wealth and living financially free, and in doing so, they developed an efficient system.

They now have multiple rental properties, as well as multiple businesses. They put in the time, they sacrificed, and they persevered. There were hiccups along the way, but by sticking with their plan they reached their goals. After planting the seeds of their future security with determination and hard work, they were finally able to reap their rewards.

# *The Wealthy Barmaid: Humble Beginnings*

My grandparents' story will always be evidence to me that working hard, saving, investing your money, and taking calculated risks really pays off. I was lucky enough to witness a variety of lessons by being around them. Even when I was young, I especially appreciated their work ethic. I practically lived with them until I started going to school; my parents literally had to pry me away because I did everything with them for years. After school started, I would only get to see them after I was out of class, and on the weekends. Needless to say, I spent a lot of time with them and we remain very close.

I started working at the age of twelve. My parents bought their own restaurant/bar in 1986, a year after I was born. When I was old enough, I worked for them and my mom taught me everything that I had to do. I was back in the kitchen at the time, which ended up being a really good learning experience for me. Typically, it was just the bartender and I working, so I was able to have some solitude in my day. I would clean, cook, and prep, and when there was downtime I would do my homework.

My mother is a master saver, which she learned from her parents. She also lived very frugally, and she taught me to save from a very young age. She would keep 100% of my paychecks, but I was really young and had no particular need for the money. When I was in high school, I held a few retail jobs, allowing me to continually grow my savings.

When I was 16 years old, I embarked on my first entrepreneurial adventure. I sold purses, jewelry, and other accessories. I would buy items wholesale from all over the place. I went to all kinds of trade shows, traveling to Toronto and Montreal to source new products. I sold these items at purse parties, festivals, and any kind of event I could get my hands on. Every part of running that business was so much fun to me, and it was a very good experience. As a young teenager, I was earning a lot of money through my entrepreneurial venture, working at the restaurant and my retail job. Through all of my hard work, I continued saving all of my earnings, and I kept watching my savings account continuously grow.

After retail, I did a few marketing jobs, which was my concentration during both my undergrad and my MBA. I took a lot of initiative in school, as soon as I saw the syllabus, by at least doing preliminary background searches or outlining projects and assignments. As opportunities arose, I volunteered regularly in each of my classes. Whenever a professor assigned a group task or a project, I took the lead arranging everything, bringing it all together and delegating tasks. I enjoyed stepping up to any challenge set forth by our professors, and as a result of my concerted effort, I graduated with honors for both of my degrees.

I believe that when we are young, we should work more toward gaining skills, experience, education, and building relationships as opposed to focusing only on the financial incentive. Children are told to go to school, then university, and then get a job. Period. Done. This is a path of life in our society.

For me, it was school, study, while also working and saving money. Then it was about taking those savings and investing it – wisely. The investment path was such a natural thing for me; it was just how my family operated. As you will learn in a few paragraphs, this willingness to invest served me well because what I initially regarded as only a safety net actually secured my future.

I started my marketing career with an agency based in Niagara. I wanted to get my feet wet, so I told them I would work three months for free. If they liked what I offered, they should hire me. If not, there would be no hard feelings and I would back away peacefully. I ended up working there for two years until I started my MBA.

I bought my first rental property at the age of twenty-two, which was an exciting venture. I discovered that I really enjoyed this process: scouting properties, negotiating with the sellers and with financial institutions to get the most desirable rates and terms, and renovating the properties themselves. To this day, I still own the first house that I bought, and it will continue to be my prized possession. While I lived there for the first few years, I did renovations, improving its value greatly. Once I finished those renovations, I started renting it out to tenants. Over the years, I found wonderful tenants, and I feel very lucky having them live there long term.

After I graduated with my MBA, I decided that I wanted a new experience, so I moved to Toronto and began hunting for a job in the corporate world. I continued working nights at a bar for extra income; after all, I had done it for so many years and I was really good at it (the money was great too). While I was in Toronto I also held a PR position which proved to be great for networking as I went to many events, and met many interesting people with whom I built great relationships and friendships. Again, I consistently saved my money while trying to keep my expenses as low as possible. Even today, I invest at least 40% of my retained earnings.

While I was in Toronto, I ended up buying another rental property. After a year in the big city, I knew it was time to start my own business. I was twenty-six and I knew the bar industry well, so I was keeping my ears open for opportunities. Within 90 days, I found one in Niagara that I really liked. Less than four months later, I purchased a 20,000-square-foot commercial property in St. Catharine's, where I started my own Gastro Pub. Owning the property was one of my long-term vision goals, and even through the hard times, it has continued to be a great business.

To this day, I continue to purchase real estate. I always keep my ear to the ground for residential and commercial properties. I am, in essence, developing an empire. I still have some way to go until I reach my goals, but because of the lessons I learned with my family, I know that this whole process has a natural progression. By implementing the strategies I have learned, and staying the course, I know that all my financial plans will come to fruition.

# The Seven Life Strategies for Becoming The Wealthy Barmaid

I feel so lucky to have embarked on my path from being a barmaid to becoming a successful entrepreneur, real estate investor, educator, hospitality business owner, author, and speaker. By implementing my family's knowledge, I have become The Wealthy Barmaid, and I want to take their philosophies and strategies to higher levels than anyone before me. As I am using these concepts to build my empire, I also want to share them with you.

The Wealthy Barmaid…

1.  Is highly disciplined
2.  Is unfazed by fear or obstacles
3.  Perseveres against all odds
4.  Passionately invests in real estate
5.  Is resourceful in securing traditional and unconventional financing
6.  Habitually grows her network
7.  Deeply values the importance of her mentors

The concept came to me in 2012 after I graduated with my MBA, while I was still bartending in Toronto, when I met a journalist at a promo event. She and I connected instantly, and we started chatting. She listened to me talk about looking for a job in marketing and that (despite my qualifications) I was having a hard time finding one amidst the recession at the time. When she learned that I had two rental properties, and that they were effectively securing my future, her interest grew to the point that she wanted to write a piece about me for The Toronto Star, Canada's largest newspaper.

She was confident that the article would inspire anyone having a hard time landing a job and securing their future. She wanted to reach out to anyone who was facing difficulty in securing financial security of any kind, regardless of what they were doing. Even though I was working nights as a bartender, and days with the PR company, I still continued to practice my investing strategies. I would never rely on any company, government, or anyone else to dictate how or when I achieved financial freedom. I would build security and wealth of my own.

When the full-page article was published in the Toronto Star, the feedback was absolutely enormous. I had thousands of people reaching out to me; all of them were fascinated by my story and wanted to know my secrets. I could not believe the kind of traction it was gaining, but because of their reaction, I realized that the concepts and strategies that I practice and follow were not second nature for everyone else. I learned that it was not on their minds to save a little money from work and invest it without any self-doubt, as opposed to always spending it, and merely living off of their earnings. It then occurred to me that there are people who are hungry for these types of stories and strategies and that they also need to feel inspired to make a change in their own lives.

I understood then that people need guidance, and I felt compelled to show others how they can build wealth and have financial freedom too. This realization encouraged me to write my full experience in a book. It encouraged me to share all the strategies and systems that I learned from family and applied to my life as I was growing up. I saw that there are people out there who are lost, and they don't know how or where to start. They don't know what they are trying to do, but they know that they want more and that they are capable of achieving more. They just have not figured out the system of doing something like this.

I want to share my story, and provide some help and guidance regardless of someone's starting point, financial situation, age, job, or credentials. There is a path to wealth, and I am living proof of this strategy. The article's response also motivated me to do something about the level of financial literacy presently available. I want to do something about all the myths that need to be crushed about money and real estate. People of all ages and backgrounds have misconceptions about what real estate is, what it can do for them, and how they can get involved. There are many misconceptions holding them back, and I want to shatter those beliefs.

I am not impressed with the education system. I do not believe that it teaches us, in any way shape or form, how to be a business person or how to run a business. The education system does not teach us how to make money, how to invest, or how to do simple banking strategies.

The current curriculum in school is not applicable to building a life that we want and securing our financial future. I want to become an activist and advocate for increasing that literacy, initiating a movement towards showing people the possibilities that really exist out there for each and every one of us.

There is no reason for anyone to live in scarcity or to sacrifice and struggle their entire lives. I want you to know that there is more out there, and that there is a simple way to do this, and I will show you how. Bringing clarity to financial security is the motivation behind my book, and I am so excited to help people just like you on this journey. I believe that you can live a life that is more fulfilling, even if you do not know where to start. Sharing this belief and my experiences with as many people as possible is now my life's purpose. Follow my strategies. Let me help you start an amazing journey. What do you have to lose?

15

*Chapter One*

# THE WEALTHY BARMAID IS HIGHLY DISCIPLINED

This all started with watching my grandparents. I was so lucky to see their habits implemented daily, and then implement them in my own life. No matter the day, they always exhibited a strong work ethic, putting in massive time and effort into pursuing their goals day after day. I remember going to the bank with them, and shopping for all kinds of supplies with them. I would hang out in the kitchen of whatever restaurant they owned at the time. My grandmother always worked with her hands, and I enjoyed helping her out with that so I would be outside with them, helping with gardening and landscaping.

On a daily basis, I saw that no matter what the day might bring, they went to work. This was their way of life. They would handle whatever needed to be handled that day. Another habit they implemented was their consistent focus on improving their businesses as well as their real estate properties. They were always adding value; in fact, they were meticulous when it came to curb appeal. Where they were from, great pride was taken in keeping home and business properties very well maintained.

They did not go to the gym, but they would purposefully do a ton of laborious activity. They had five acres at their house where they farmed, mowed, and did maintenance. They had animals and took good care of them, and had a pond with fish. My grandfather made a patio all by himself – the base, the deck and railings, everything. Inside their house, they redid the flooring by themselves, and revamped both the bathroom and the kitchen.

Over breakfast, any meal, midnight snack or a late-night coffee, I would listen to them discussing business. They would brainstorm entertainment, and whether they wanted a live band or a DJ on a busy night. I heard them discussing any sports teams they should acquire or create. They would consider teams in billiards, chess, and darts; anything they could make into an in-house league. My grandparents also discussed possible tournaments to attract business. Of course, they would also discuss expenses and which ones could be cut back as well.

Most importantly, my grandparents never stopped believing in themselves and their abilities. No matter what they set out to do, they never doubted that they have what it takes to accomplish it. Certainly, fear will come in at some point – for all of us – but if you are in the midst of pursuing something and you sit and worry about it all day long, you will waste time that could be spent more effectively towards the objective.

Confidence is your greatest asset. Your ability to do anything (especially challenging things) is more a reflection of your *level of confidence* than it is your actual ability, and it determines:

- The size of the challenges and goals you undertake
- How likely you are to achieve those goals
- How well you bounce back from failures

If you are not confident, you will never put yourself out there in the first place. When you are confident, you will not care how many times you fail; you know you will succeed. It will not matter how stacked the odds seem against you.

My grandparents would not let fear or vulnerability stop them or hold them back from anything. They became successful because they kept pushing and taking risks. Their belief in themselves has always been rock solid. Because of them, I believe it is important to learn that you can accomplish anything. It is important that you develop and nurture that belief in yourself.

They were also very good at managing their money. They never over-consumed, and they lived very frugally. I feel that they learned a lot from their life in the former Yugoslavia. I think it taught them about valuing their money. Immigrants often learn how to take care of their money and value it more so than most of us do in North America. My grandparents still live frugally, fixing things versus throwing them out or buying replacements, and staying home and cooking instead of eating out at a restaurant. Their costs are purposefully still kept very low, which is an important strategy of building wealth that I was exposed to early on.

They were definitely from a different era. Things have changed since they grew up, since they were conditioned to be like this, but the concept still applies. They will not charge anything to their credit cards when they know they can afford it in cash. They always save a large portion of their earnings (30% to 40%) when they can, and they invest those savings into businesses or real estate in order to get ahead. Managing money is one of the most important concepts to learn when you are trying to build wealth.

# *10 Habits of a Wealthy Barmaid*

Many of the topics I cover are behavioral and changing behavior is never easy. In fact, the first part of this book is all about you, and who you need to become in order to be successful. Being disciplined is what it takes in order to build wealth and to reach and enjoy your financial freedom. Some of what I cover in this chapter might be simple, so if you feel that you already know some of it, great, but ask yourself: Do I actually put this into effect?

Do you put any of these habits into action? Your willingness to put in that effort and do something is what makes all the difference. This willingness will either keep you where you are today or make your goals become a reality.

These habits are ones that I implement daily. I believe that each of them is critical on the road to building wealth:

1. Keep your mind strong
2. Keep your body strong
3. Cultivate a strong work ethic
4. Set clear goals and visualize
5. Manage your money meticulously
6. Surround yourself with likeminded/motivated people
7. Manage your time with purpose
8. Add value to your ventures
9. Make decisions quickly & <u>always take action</u>
10. Be consistent

# 1. Keep Your Mind Strong

Control your emotions. Be careful not to make emotional decisions, especially by keeping negative thoughts out of your surroundings. We all have crummy days, but the goal is to not stay in that state for long. When tiredness and general frustration seeps into our lives, it is important that we not let it stay, whether it is an actual event or waking up on the wrong side of the bed. Reminding yourself to stay out of that state can be difficult, so it is important to remember that no matter what that pain might be, it is temporary. Your growth, progress, and dreams cannot suffer because there was a blip in the road. You must condition this mindset like a muscle.

Life will not always go the way that you want it to, but when it comes down to it, you have the same twenty-four hours as everyone else. Successful people do their best to make their time count. Instead of complaining about how things could have been or should have been, they reflect on everything that they are grateful for in their life. Then they find the best solution available, tackle the problem, and move forward.

## Never Give Up

This is absolutely crucial for conditioning. There will be many times throughout your investing and business career when you want to throw in the towel. When things get sticky, you will find yourself wanting to sell it all and just quit. If you want to build wealth, you should never allow setbacks to take you off course, deflating everything you are trying to build and achieve.

There have been many people in my life who have given into this fear in the past. Some of them had a horrible tenant situation and they said, "Forget this. It's not for me." They said it was ridiculous and unfair how the legal system operates, and how people treated their property. They made their exit and moved on with their lives.

I had some serious tenant issues myself. I later learned they were literally con artists who fooled me, costing me thousands of dollars. Adding insult to injury, they were very unpleasant throughout the whole incident. Going through the legal process of removing them was lengthy, costly, and frustrating. I paid out of pocket to stay afloat with that property. However, I did not let myself give up, nor did I give in, nor did I get out of the business. It was a learning experience.

I kept pushing through that moment because I knew those con artists were just a bump in the road. I learned my lesson from that experience, and currently I am much more rigorous with tenant screenings. I know from sticking to my goals and pushing myself through the hard times, without allowing any one situation destroy me, that in the long run this will make me more successful.

## Believe in Yourself

Having confidence is important; you must never doubt yourself. When you believe in yourself, an amazing thing happens: the people around you start believing in you too. You need to own your abilities, capabilities, talents, skills, and competencies. Once you own these aspects of yourself, you will have faith in yourself, and everyone else will too. It is perfectly fine if you are not an expert quite yet. It is only human if you have not 100% mastered any particular ability of yours. If you are determined to continue making that grow, to build that up, this determination is all you need.

When I became a business owner, I needed to exude confidence in my craft; running the business itself, managing my staff, and dealing with customers, suppliers, and vendors. I was able to create a successful business by being confident in myself and my abilities. My experiences have shown me that in order to succeed you need to sustain a rock-solid belief in what you do, as well as how you do it. You need to be confident even when you are facing self-doubt.

## *Acquire Knowledge Daily*

Knowledge works like building blocks; like compound interest. We all have the capacity to grow very successful by changing our daily habits little by little. There are tons of resources out there, and some of them are free thanks to the internet. There are also books, seminars, courses, industry publications, lectures, and interviews. Knowledge will be your best friend always, in any interest.

I love reading because I am hungry to learn how things work. I like reading biographies of successful people for inspiration and guidance. I also love books on specific topics like real estate, the stock market, entrepreneurism, or leadership. I enjoy reading whatever and wherever it is that I want to increase my knowledge in. I learn something new every time I read; it grows and expands my brain.

Not only does reading make you well rounded as an individual, it also allows you to explore and learn new concepts. It is an activity that introduces you to other things you may not have known previously. Reading can help develop your skillset, and make you more valuable in the marketplace.

Something major that the world's most successful people have in common is that they read a lot, because books are a gateway to learning and knowledge. Some extremely successful people never had a formal education, nor did they earn any degrees, but reading was a way for them to continuously learn. Reading is a key ingredient to their success. While anyone can grab a book and read it, I guarantee you that not all people will.

# 2. *Keep Your Body Strong*

This habit helps your mind, reduces stress, and gives you energy to pursue your dreams and goals. By staying active, you will have more energy to work harder. Personally, I have always been physically active. I was a competitive gymnast for fifteen years, during which time I developed a fundamental enjoyment of hard physical activity. I have always felt the need to stay active and strong, and I notice that when I am not exerting my body or continuously working on it, I do not feel strong and clear minded. I also noticed that my whole body and mentality will reflect this feeling. Today, I have a trainer, I enjoy some extreme sports, and I do fun and challenging physical activities.

These activities continue giving energy to me for working harder throughout the day. Activity keeps me motivated and clear headed, not to mention it feels good and keeps me entertained. I love challenging myself and seeing my capabilities, so I have always been active. I also know that it is so easy to become lazy if we refrain from doing anything physical for a little while, so I learned early on that for me to operate at full capacity in business, it is important to keep my body in peak physical shape.

# 3. Cultivate a Strong Work Ethic

Being wealthy requires effort, as anything worth having does. You need to be willing to invest your time and effort for greater prosperity. This is an investment in a better life, one that you desire. Day after day, year after year, you should be constantly working towards whatever it is that you want. I always maintain my strong work ethic by working hard, and working consistently.

No matter how I feel on any given day, I get up and I go to work. I do not take sick days. I do not stay indoors because I don't feel like going to work, or because I just feel lousy that day. I always make an effort to work harder on myself and my businesses every single day.

Absolutely, there are days when I do not feel like going to work. However, once I get myself going, I feel more like pushing forward. I feel better and energized once I am in the thick of it, as I progress closer to my goals. On the flip side, if I took a day to sit at home, watching television, it would feel like a wasted day. I know that I will not have progressed any closer to my goals, and due to my lack of action on that particular day, nothing new will happen tomorrow, or a week from now, or next year, and so on.

My grandfather always told me, "Sometimes we have to do things we don't feel like doing if we want to succeed, or get better at something." It is very important that you maintain your work ethic. Keep it strong, work constantly, and be diligent towards whatever it is you are pursuing.

# 4. Set Clear Goals and Visualize

I always knew that I had a lot of potential. I wanted to do more, and I knew I had more within myself to offer. I always wanted more money, freedom, and time, but did not specify my goals clearly enough early in my path. Regrettably, it took me a while to figure out that the path would stay blurry if I did not have a very clear outcome or objective. Saying that you want to make $100,000 through real estate in the next two years is a goal. Saying you want to be rich is not.

Having goals that are clearly defined as well as time bound will ensure that you reach them. Do not solely be a daily goal setter, but also be a daily goal hitter. What you do today greatly affects whether or not you will achieve your future dreams. You need to intentionally design each and every day in a way that leads to getting things done, in a way that maximizes your results. By this I do not just mean making yourself busy every minute of the day just for the sake of being busy. It is important to know what is important and then focus on those things.

Having this concrete goal with a timeline attached is how you will be able to start taking action towards it. However, do not think too far into the future. Things change frequently over time. Set a clear goal, or else you will not know what you are after. You will constantly search for something that may never happen, and you may never find it. There is nothing worse than feeling lost or lacking a clear direction as to where you want your life to go. This is why I believe that visualizing is important. With my goals, I find that it helps immensely.

I close my eyes and envision the situation that I will be in, whether it be my next meeting or my next negotiation over a deal. I envision how it will go, and what the process will look like. I envision what objectives I might receive. Visualizing not only brings me confidence, but it is also great for preparation; which usually works in your favor. There will be some bumps along the way, there will be obstacles for which you need to prepare, and visualizing is a great way to get where you need to go with more velocity.

# 5. Manage Your Money Meticulously

Step 1: You have to earn it.

Step 2: (almost as important as the first step) You have to save it.

Do not over consume. To build wealth, you need to want to be wealthy, and to have greater prosperity you must avoid that urge to spend everything that you earn. You need to track and budget how much you make, and you need to know how much you will save in order to invest it in the future. I recommend setting aside <u>at least</u> 20% of your earnings, and living below your means.

You need to practice financial diligence by keeping track of what is coming in and what is going out. Many people do not know these numbers and this works against them. It is important that you get very specific about what you have coming in from all your income sources. You also need to know exactly what is going out. Sometimes you will not realize how much of your money is going out because of little things like magazine subscriptions or gym memberships. Write every single thing down and then curb your spending, so that you can put a portion aside for investing.

My strategy has been more aggressive than putting aside 20% for as long as I can remember. There was a time when I was putting 100% of my paychecks aside and a portion of my tips as well. Currently, I save and invest at least 40% of my earnings annually. As I do this, I know that I am doing it for the betterment of my future. I am not going without, mind you, but I also do not feel the need to over consume and spend every penny I make.

My money is hard earned, so I want to see it working for me rather than the other way around. This is why I invest. In order to become wealthy, you must start thinking in terms of your net worth, and not just your income. This distinction is an important component to building wealth.

A distinguishing feature of people who achieve wealth is that they manage their money extremely well. They do not necessarily earn the most. They are neither the smartest in the world, nor did they go through any special training. They just have really good money habits. You need to adopt these kinds of habits to serve your wealth goals. In order to adopt this habit, you need to be honest with yourself: Where do you stand exactly?

If you are a little behind, then you need to resolve, in this moment, that you are declaring a war on that debt. When you make your declaration, you then need to commit to getting rid of it. Not all of us are at the same starting point, and that is okay. If you have debt that needs to be cleared up before you can start investing and building wealth, I have an appendix in this book for you. Therein I have written out strategies for getting rid of your debt. I have also laid out strategies for you to speed up the process so you can begin the road to building wealth much faster. For those of you who are ready for the jump, whose debts are cleared up and who are ready to go, now is the time to begin that road.

## *Net Worth Statement*

If I asked you what your net worth is right now, would you be able to answer me on the spot? Most people do not calculate their net worth, nor do they even know where they stand on the topic. If they do not know that information, how do they know if they are growing or not?

I want you to keep a personal balance sheet, a Net Worth Statement. My recommendation is that you look at it at least quarterly, because you will need to measure your progress. When you follow the strategies shared in this book, you will see that number steadily increase. I do this all the time, writing everything down, and looking at my net worth statement constantly. If I make any major purchases, I update it. If I accomplish any goals or acquire more assets, I adjust it.

This is the whole idea, increasing our net worth. I want you to make thinking net worth a habit, and then I want you to get excited about trying to build this on a daily basis. Over time, condition yourself to think about finding solutions to making your net worth grow. The more solutions you find, and the more honest you are with yourself, the more you will have a real understanding of how wealth is built, and how it will affect your financial position.

---

**An example of how to make a Net Worth statement:**

Take a blank sheet of paper, and draw a line down the middle. On the left side, list off all of your assets. These are things that you own:

- Real estate
- Cash in your bank accounts
- Investments
- RRSP's, TFSA, Bonds, etc.
- Value of vehicles you own
- Tally up the total worth of all these things.

On the right side, list all of your liabilities. These are the things that you owe:

- Mortgages remaining on any properties
- Credit card balances
- Lines of credit
- School loans
- Vehicle loans
- Add up the total worth of all these things as well.

$$\boxed{\text{Net Worth} = \text{Assets} - \text{Liabilities}}$$

I have included an example of a Net Worth Statement in the appendix at the end of this book for you to use as a tool. Keep your statement on hand so that you can regularly update it. The more accessible it is, the easier it will be to remember revising it.

# 6. Surround Yourself with Likeminded/Motivated People

Ideally, you need to meet people who are already where you want to be. The more you put yourself out there and see what others are doing, as well as how they are doing it, the more it will expand your mind and help you grow. A network will give you inspiration, ideas, encouragement, and hope. It will also help you stay focused on your goals when you see and are around others who are trying to do something meaningful with their lives.

It is inspiring to be around go-getters who have grand visions for their futures and current lives. Personally, I go to a ton of events. I find whatever I can get my hands on, both free and paid. I will attend meet-up seminars, networking groups, investment clubs, conferences, and training boot camps, etc. Sometimes I will not be in the mood to drive to Toronto (where most of these events are, near me), due to so many hours spent in traffic, but I will still push myself to go. The feeling completely changes once I arrive because the people and the ideas that I am exposed to inspire and excite me. The overall experience gives me a motivational boost.

Networks also help me get comfortable being uncomfortable. It takes me out of my limited comfort zone to learn something new that I can apply in my life. These events help in meeting lots of new and interesting people too. Yes, going into a room full of strangers can be very uncomfortable. Yes, when you do not know anyone, it can feel very awkward and scary being in attendance. However, the more often that you put yourself out there, the better your chances of success will become. We will not make it in this world alone. Nobody has made anything completely by themselves. People are your greatest resource.

Not every event will be amazing or yield fantastic results, but some of them just might spark something inside of you. The more you network, the more you will find opportunities to build relationships with people who might propel you into a new phase of your life. You never know who you will meet or the connections that you can make. These connections are not only for the betterment of your financial and your business life, but for your personal life as well.

## *Keep Mentors and Coaches*

I have found myself a few coaches over the years. I find that it is very valuable to have someone guiding me and holding me accountable to all my goals and progress. It is also great having someone around to bounce ideas and strategies off of; someone who has already accomplished the things I want to do, who has been to the places I want to go. A mentor or coach allows navigation through ventures or industries without making very costly mistakes. They also help by giving insight to me, shortcuts that I may never have known about if I proceeded blind or alone.

It is incredibly motivating to acquire perspective from someone who can get you where you want to go, and who will get you there faster. Time is of the essence. The quicker you get to where you want to go, the better off you will be, and the more you will have around you to enjoy. The world's wealthiest people have coaches; very few people operate in a bubble. There always comes a time when you plateau in whatever business or career you are doing, and a coach is the one person who can get you to the next level.

Getting insight and guidance from someone who is operating at a higher level will help you navigate the best steps in moving forward. The right mentor can take you to that next stage, whereas without their guidance you would have remained right where you were before meeting them. You might stay in limbo because you do not know what your next step is, or how you need to do it.

You need to push yourself through that threshold of leaving your comfort zone, and getting out of that can be scary, but having a mentor or coach propels you into taking the necessary actions. In the interest of getting to wherever you are trying to go, they will help you to accomplish this safely, securely, and with more wisdom at your side. Because of this, coaches and mentors are both key ingredients for success.

# 7. Manage Your Time with Purpose

I am a big believer in not wasting time watching television, surfing the web, or perusing social media in any of my spare time. Nor am I a believer in doing any of these things in my productive hours during the day. There is only so much time per diem, and time is our greatest asset, so I try to use it for personal development: building skills, learning new things, new industries, working on side projects, or developing my current ventures and businesses. You should also use this time to better yourself into the person you want to be.

I rarely watch television. I never feel any need to watch something without lessons, aside from an outing like going to the movies. I do not waste precious time on sitcoms or reality shows, because these things will give me nothing during the time that I could spend building my empire. What we choose to do with our time vastly influences where we end up in life. As an ambitious person, I am always left feeling like there are still things left to do. If I could clone myself (if only), I would get so much more work done.

There is not enough time in the day for you to get lost in the ocean of surfing the internet or television channels. You will get more accomplished if you spend that time building your empire and bettering yourself. Without question, we are all living in the most distracted time in human history, where remaining focused on a single task is nearly impossible for more than a few minutes at a time. While most of the world is becoming increasingly distracted, a select few are capitalizing on this fact. When something sucks, do you give up? OR do you push through and eventually enjoy the satisfaction of growth and success?

Anything worth doing or having will be rough at some point, and that is the problem facing most people nowadays. We used to sacrifice momentary pleasure for a better future, but the overpowering message of today is to "live for the moment." This is exactly what people do today; they live for this moment, and when something does not go as planned or it becomes difficult, most people will quit. A majority of us will indulge ourselves in momentary satisfaction at the expense of a better future. Doing the work is hard, but you can absolutely learn to endure the discomfort of the moment to build a life worth living.

## *Avoid Procrastination*

Start before you are ready.

Just as today's majority of people enjoy indulging in momentary or impulsive actions and simple pleasures, so too will that majority wait (and wait...) when their consequences are perceived as dire. They believe in not starting anything until they have "enough time," "more money," "stronger connections," or "better credentials." They wait until they feel "secure."

This waiting is not a trait of the successful and the wealthy. Determined people started last year. They started five years ago, before they even knew what they were doing. They started before they even had the money. They started before they had every answer, and when no one else believed in them. The only permission they needed was the inner voice prompting them to move forward. They felt prompted and so they moved.

When you know what you are after, and what you are working towards, do not wait in any way for perfection, because it will never happen. You need to jump in and get started. Even when the concept of this book initially crossed my mind, and building The Wealthy Barmaid brand, many thoughts held me back from bringing it to fruition. *There is no way*, I thought, *that I can write a book. I am not a writer. Will my story and message actually help anyone out there?*

I kept putting my book off until I was reminded by one of my coaches that by avoiding it, I was cheating not only myself but others as well. I was cheating others of having access to my story and message. I was cheating them of the resources and inspiration that may help in achieving their financial freedom and wealth. I was then reminded that by helping just one person, my efforts would be worth every minute spent, and every word written. I was worrying over every little detail before diving into the process, so I decided to stop being a perfectionist. I knew that I needed to keep going and learn everything as I went along.

Nothing is ever exactly how you want it to be, especially in those beginning stages. Do not hold yourself back by procrastinating, because (particularly with regard to investing) procrastination is the single biggest wealth killer. Time is your best friend and asset. While you might plan on getting around to it someday, in the meantime there are always other expenses and obstacles.

If you just keep waiting and waiting, nothing positive will ever happen. There will always be some other priority if you allow it. Your mentality and actions will either keep you exactly where you are today, or they will take you where you want to be tomorrow.

## *Plan Your Day the Night Before*

This helps you stay on point with your goals. Planning your day the night before will keep you moving forward consistently. You should do things every day that progress you closer to success. This is not about keeping a traditional to-do list or something that keeps you busy all day long, because this can be unproductive. I suggest you focus on the actual outcome, and then do things daily that specifically bring you closer to reaching your goal. Even if you set the goals, if you are not focused and working on what is important now, you will not succeed.

Successful people know what is important in the moment, and they are relentless in getting it done. They do not allow themselves to get distracted by unimportant stuff. Successful people possess an ability to stay focused when others are not, which is no easy feat the higher up you move within an organization (or the more involved you become as an entrepreneur) because everyone wants a piece of your attention. If you want to be successful, you need to develop the discipline to not let anything take your focus from the important things that bring results. Sure, it takes a lot of practice as you develop that discipline, but at the end of the day those results are absolutely worth your hard work.

Every night I go through my calendar and I look at what I am doing the next day. If there are flexible tasks, I schedule the most important ones during the time that I am the most productive. Some of us are morning people, and others are night people. In order to fully utilize my creative energies, I ensure that I get those tasks done during the day when I am at my peak state.

Planning this way also helps me prepare and prioritize mentally. I hate waking up to a million different things that I have to do. I hate waking up when it all feels insurmountable because I never planned it out. However, because I plan it out, I hit the ground running in the morning. By planning my day the night before, I know what I will be doing, which keeps me on track and moving forward effectively and efficiently.

The more you are planning ahead, the less you will allow random things to pop up and keep you from pursuing what needs to be done. Everything can distract you, so it is important to keep your schedule as tight as you possibly can. Allow no distractions in today because they keep you from reaching your goals tomorrow. Establishing these repetitive habits, leading to effective performance, is the key to winning results. Your outcome is what truly matters and you need to be laser focused on it.

# 8. Add Value to Your Ventures

Going above and beyond in all your ventures is really important for adding value to your endeavors. At work, you need to do everything you can to make things better. You have to find ways of working more efficiently, to add more value, and to be more productive in a given day. Try to learn new or better ways to do what you are already doing. Try to offer more value or services to your current industry, business, or job.

For example, I added live entertainment nights to my gastro pub. I hosted more parties and special events, and I created promotions. These additions brought happy repeat customers, as well as an increase in sales, because I was going above and beyond. I was providing an exciting evening out for locals, and regardless of the event, I thought outside of the box. I could have remained a "regular" restaurant/bar open from 11 am to 10 pm, serving food and drinks, but I wanted to take it beyond that. I wanted to create value and something more for customers to enjoy.

With my real estate investments, I do not just sign a lease with the tenants, hand them the key, and hope they never call me again with any issues. Again, I learned from my network, my real estate agent, and from going to events: <u>Go above and beyond.</u> I make it a point to bring my tenants gift baskets when I welcome them to their new house. I help them with anything that they need in order to make the place feel like home. I stay in touch, and make sure they do not need anything.

I am extremely responsive and whenever they do need anything; I address their concerns immediately. I go above and beyond by bringing the little things to my tenants: holiday gifts on special occasions, little trinkets, and cards to show my gratitude. I develop relationships with my tenants. I add value to our deal, and they love living in my houses because I go above and beyond what anyone would expect from a typical landlord. Most of my tenants stay with me for many years, and they cause no hassle for me.

Again, adding value comes down to thinking unconventionally and applying any knowledge that you have learned from others. You can enhance your ventures through creativity, and by implementing what you learn. This combination is the secret of going above and beyond what is expected of you. You will find success through these efforts before long.

While you add value, avoid the mindset of things being above your pay grade. You need to care, and avoid the thought that you are doing "enough." "Enough" is not a productive mentality. Nobody pays for average or mediocre, so you need to keep adding value to everything that you do.

# 9. *Make Decisions Quickly & Always Take Action*

After making a decision, without taking action nothing ever happens. <u>You are where you are today because of your past decisions</u>. Look at your surroundings, and let that sink in for a minute. Look at your career, where you live, your relationships, and your income. For some, this statement might be a cold hard slap in the face, and for others this might bring a feeling of pride from where they have been in order to arrive where they are today.

It is not enough to simply have a dream. You need to actively pursue it. Most people who talk endlessly about dreams but never do anything to pursue them are effectively choosing not to choose. They end up with a life they do not recognize, and they wonder why they feel so beaten down and defeated. However, deep down they know they have another choice. The truth is that over the long term, you only have one good option: <u>Own your dream</u>. If you refuse to, you will become a tenant in someone else's dream.

I made many decisions to be where I am today. For example with my teenage entrepreneurial venture, when I decided to start selling purses and accessories, I made a decision, I followed through, and I was successful at it. Another example is when I bought my first house at twenty-two, as well as buying my first commercial property at twenty-seven. Both decisions greatly affected my life.

Personally, I think my scariest decision was to run my gastro pub. However, I did not debate it for very long, because I had to make a decision quickly. As a result of immediately taking action, I am where I am today. Without taking action, I would have just discussed and debated it forever, and nothing would have happened.

Speed of implementation is what determines the level of success that someone will achieve. Respond immediately rather than analyzing and stalling. Just do it. Train yourself to respond immediately whenever you need to take action. Stop questioning yourself or over-analyzing – just act. You will figure out what you need to do <u>after</u> you have taken action. Until you take action, everything is hypothetical. However, once you act, it becomes practical.

I do not believe in circumstances, but many people blame them for where they are today. I hope that you are not that person. I concede that we do not all start on a level playing field and have the same access to opportunity. However, I also believe that you are not defined by your starting position. I believe in working hard, and taking action.

I hope you believe in either finding the circumstances you want, or creating them. Blaming people around you, your surroundings, or giving excuses for where you are today is a waste of time. Do not do it.

# 10. Be Consistent

The importance of consistency in business seems so basic that it doesn't need discussion. Yet many companies, especially smaller ones, operate in a day-by-day, case-by-case fashion. This can be disorganized, undisciplined, and inefficient. This does not breed trust with your customers, clients, or fellow business associates. Even the best business plans will fail without any dedication to consistency.

If I say I will do something, I will do it. If I say I will be somewhere, then I will be there. When I initiate a new business process or initiative, I will follow through no matter what. In my experience, consistency is a must as you build and grow both your business and your reputation.

Until you have tried something new in a consistent manner for a period of time, you cannot decide if it actually works. How do you measure effectiveness if what you are measuring is not performed consistently? Personally, I ask employees to be accountable for their deliverables and goals. I believe that they should expect the same in return from my leadership, so I make it a priority to have time for and be available to my team.

Consistency means providing predictable, reliable results to the customer, client, partner, or associate every time you do business with them. Consistency itself creates the reputation on which your business will be built. Without it, you will find yourself constantly learning from mistakes that you really cannot afford to make, and the customers who leave you will give no indication as to why.

You achieve consistency by doing the same thing in the same way, because it produces the same result each and every time you do it. When maintaining investment properties, it is important how your contractors treat your tenants or your partners. This is important because it is a direct reflection of you and how you do business. Develop standard procedures for day-to-day interactions with clients, customers, and business associates to help create a consistent experience. Make sure that you never make a promise you cannot keep. You should always strive to exceed the customer's or client's expectations.

From the way your business looks, the way your team treats clients and customers, to how well you keep the promises you make to them, the only way to get the consistency you need to achieve the results you want is to develop procedures that will give you consistent results. You need to hold yourself and your team to these standards.

In my hospitality business, I always stress consistency. I make sure that my hours of operation are consistent. I have communication procedures with the teams I sponsor, as well as the live entertainment that we schedule. I do not want potential customers wondering whether we will be open at a certain time. They should not wonder if a particular promotion or event is still happening, or if they should make the trip out to my establishment late at night. If people have too many questions, then I did not do my job well.

Too many times I have gone to bars/restaurants and because they are so inconsistent with their hours of operation, I stop going. Many businesses wing it, and this is obvious to their customers as they only stay open as long as they are busy. Customers stop going because the doors open and close at different times day to day and week to week. In business, you must be consistent across the board for long-term success.

# *Before We Begin*

Nothing will change unless you do. This book is more about you as a person than it is about money. You are the instrument that makes the money, and it is much harder to manage yourself than it is to manage your finances. If I were to take you under my wing and to train you intensely one on one for any span of time to make you wealthy, I would need to know:

- Do you have what it takes to be wealthy?
- Are you determined enough?
- Will you work hard enough?
- Will you stick with it?
- Do you have the stamina?
- Do you have relentless focus?

If these things are not a part of you then you will not succeed, and we will both have wasted our time. These models and habits are focused on acquiring some serious financial wealth in your life. Remember that good habits put money in your pocket, while bad habits take money out and drag you down. If your goals are not crystal clear right from the start, then you will feel lost because you will not know what you are pursuing. If you do not know what you are after, then you will never reach an outcome.

There were times when I felt lost, and I was unsure of where I was going. I felt unclear about what I was trying to do and what my purpose was overall. There have been times when I was unsure of how I would make money or secure myself financially. There were also times when I was unsure about how I could make myself feel safer. In these times, I focused on developing habits and embracing the strategies that kept me moving forward.

When you are a little lost, when the destination is not clear, you will end up running in circles. If you implement these habits daily, they will help you stay the course. When all of them are a part of your routine, you will reach your destination much faster than you would have without them. In the words of Benjamin Franklin:

"Your net worth is usually determined by what remains after your bad habits are subtracted from your good ones."

# *Chapter Highlights*

- Read as often as possible.
- Keep yourself physically strong.
- Set a strong work ethic and stick to it.
- Set clear goals.
- Be diligent about your money:
- Keep track of what goes in and what goes out.
- Curb the urge to spend it all.
- Put a certain portion aside for investing.
- Surround yourself with positive people.
- Procrastination is the single biggest wealth killer.
- You must undoubtedly believe in yourself and your capabilities.
- Enhance your ventures by adding value.
- Make decisions and take action frequently.
- Good habits put money in your pocket.
- Bad habits take money out and drag you down.

## The Formula for Wealth:
[Small, Smart Choices] x [Consistency] x [Time] = Wealth

*Chapter 2*

# THE WEALTHY BARMAID IS UNFAZED BY FEAR OR OBSTACLES

The biggest obstacle within your full control is <u>you</u>. Fear and self-doubt are crippling if you allow them to be, but if you conquer them, your whole life and your business will change for the better. The obstacles faced by my grandparents when they left safety and security in the former Yugoslavia, and the way they continually pushed themselves towards their goals, will always be a shining example to me of conquering fear and self-doubt. They spoke zero English. They had no jobs and no security. They had no place to live, no particular skills, no money, and no training or education. Still, with all these obstacles, they kept moving forward towards their eventual success.

My grandfather once decided to take an opportunity at a brand-new, large factory hiring welders. He knew nothing about welding, but he decided to apply for the job anyway because this factory was paying significantly better than the one where he was currently working. The increase would be a big step up for him and his family, and he would stop at nothing to get it. The morning that the application process opened, he went there ready to land that job.

When he arrived, the line for applicants was over two miles long! The average person would probably lose all motivation upon seeing that line, but not my grandpa. He saw opportunity. He quickly went back home, changed into his suit, and grabbed his tie and his briefcase. When he returned to the factory, he did not wait in line. He passed everyone and walked straight to the front with such an air of confidence that nobody stopped him.

The hiring managers took him into their office right away for an interview. When they asked my grandfather how many years of welding experience he had, he told them ten! They hired him on the spot. His new job paid $6.00 an hour, whereas his previous job had only paid $1.75. This was a 243% wage increase! He was so excited at the prospect.

He remembers to this day how horrible he was at welding, especially because he had no experience. The supervisor eventually took him aside, and asked him again about his experience with welding. Of course, my grandpa had to tell the truth. He explained how he, his wife, and their two kids had just arrived in Canada. This job was necessary for him to take care of his family, so he told the supervisor that he was a quick learner, and that he would work day and night to get it right.

The supervisor liked his determination. He told my grandfather that he needed more people like him on his team. He ended up personally training him how to properly weld on the side. My grandfather picked it up immediately, and after one year they promoted him to Lead Hand Man.

Besides being a fast learner, he was a really hard worker – all of this was in his background and his upbringing. It was how his parents taught him in the old country. My grandfather was refreshing to his bosses, and they took a strong liking to him because of his work ethic. Another year after that, they offered him a foreman position, which he did not take because he knew that he wanted to go into business for himself. He ended up doing exactly that shortly after turning down their offer.

The moral of this story is that with every solution my grandfather came to, he did not see any obstacles as setbacks; he instead saw each of them as an opportunity. My grandparents hit the ground running, and they would both figure it out as they went along. Failure was not an option as they both continually earned money, and kept looking for new and better ways to earn it. As they made more money, they continuously put it into their savings account, and as that increased they also started investing.

By spending so much time with my grandparents, I saw that nothing goes as planned. No venture goes perfectly smooth from start to finish; there are bumps along the way. One night when I was sleeping at their house, it was very late, and they got a call from their restaurant/bar. Something had been broken, or there was a fight, so they scooped me up, wrapped a blanket around me, and we went to see what went wrong, and what they could do about it.

I watched them figure it all out, and no matter the emergency, they would stay calm. They were always level-headed. They would assess whatever happened, and they would either find a solution or call the appropriate authorities.

My father would sometimes see an alarm going off from his business, and he would go check it out no matter what was going on, or what time it was. I remember him waking up at three in the morning very often. My family always does whatever it takes to keep moving forward. They showed me how to fight through the storms. They taught me the mentality needed to get tough, and to push through all obstacles. They taught me how to understand that in life, things do not always go up.

There are times when things get rough, and you need to get through it. You need to push harder if you must, or you need to wait out the storms. I grew up with the understanding that markets fluctuate, people do not always deliver, and things will not always work out as planned.

Another important aspect to consider is my grandparents' major introspection. Their self-talk was positive and confident. Without question, they believed in themselves and they owned their abilities. They had no choice other than putting this belief into their heads. They knew what they were setting out to do, and they knew what was necessary for them to accomplish it.

My grandparents regularly took action, and they saw opportunities in situations where most people would not. When they faced any kind of setback, they would adopt a new strategy and figure things out as they went along. They would always seek new solutions in the midst of any given obstacle, just as it is said of entrepreneurs:

> You jump out of the plane,
> and you build a parachute
> on the way down.

# *Entrepreneurial Obstacles*

These obstacles are commonly faced by entrepreneurs. The sooner you pass seemingly insurmountable obstacles, the sooner you will reach your goals, and attain the wealth and freedom you desire and deserve. I see these entrepreneurial obstacles as the most important to keep in mind:

1. Fear and self-doubt
2. Abandoning security
3. Raising capital
4. Maintaining focus
5. Managing people
6. Making decisions

# *1. Fear and Self-Doubt*

Fear is nothing more than a lingering emotion fueled by your imagination. Danger is very real, on the other hand: It's the uncomfortable rush of adrenaline that you get when you almost step in front of a bus. Where danger is a reaction, fear is a choice. Never hold back in life just because you feel scared. I often hear people say, "What's the worst thing that can happen to you? Will it kill you?" But death isn't the worst thing that can happen to you. The worst thing that can happen to you is allowing yourself to die inside while you are still alive.

Everyone has fears, and it requires discipline to acknowledge them for yourself, and then determine if they are valid. One technique for facing your fears is to write each of them down, no matter how big or small. Then for each fear listed, write down the worst-case scenario if that fear became a reality. You might find that they are not nearly as bad as you expected. The goal is to see things as they really are - not worse than they are.

If you have not figured it out by now, you will have to change not only your actions, but also the way you see the world. If you were not in need of change you would not be reading this book. Changes in finances and freedom begin with changes in your thoughts, and they end with changing your actions.

There have been many times in the past when I have doubted myself and my capabilities. I found myself thinking that I was not good or smart enough. I worried that I would be unable to learn or execute new things, or that I didn't know enough about a particular industry. Often, I found myself wondering if others were doing everything better than me, and I have certainly asked myself, "How can I possibly compete?"

As it turned out, feelings like these are not uncommon. Some studies show that 70% of humanity experiences persistent feelings of inadequacy, self-doubt, and intellectual fraudulence. This has been named the Imposter Syndrome, and it runs rampant among high achievers. Some might simply chalk it up to being humble, but living life constantly wallowing in self-doubt, and second-guessing our abilities can hold us back significantly from reaching our dream levels of success. Self-doubt holds us hostage and impedes important work. It causes procrastination as well as playing it small, rather than pursuing big opportunities that may have a big impact.

As I learned to early on, I persuaded myself that I had potential. I owed it to myself to break through my fears of inadequacy and the possibility of failure. I owed myself proof that I could be successful. I never would have found the courage to make any attempt (let alone get somewhere) in business or real estate without this mindset. I would have ended up with nothing, because for my entire life I would have played it safe, and I would have stayed in my narrow comfort zone. At the end of it all, I never would have achieved anything. Instead, I learned how to face my fears.

I remember the week before my deal closed on my first commercial property in 2013. I lost so much sleep from tossing and turning my way through all my worry and negative self-talk. I was so worried about my ability to own a gastro pub, run the bar, provide a full-service restaurant, and maintain a huge property. In a matter of days, this decision would become real, and my goodness, you should have heard the things I was telling myself.

*There is no way that a twenty-seven-year-old girl is capable of running a huge operation such as this one all by herself.* For so many nights, I was crunching numbers from every possible angle. *I will fail, no doubt, and be the laughingstock of my family and the community around me.* I ran through how much I needed to make in sales, and how fast I needed to grow. *I will prove them all right and be a failure.* I had a friend who would come over each and every time I called her, and we would go over my plan countless times. We discussed teams just like my grandparents did, tournaments, and live events, brainstorming anything that we thought would guarantee an increase in business.

I could not stop going over everything because I was so determined not to fail. Even worse, everyone thought I would fail too, close friends and family alike. This was a huge test, but it was also one that changed my life forever. I worried myself sick. I was scared out of my mind and the feeling was awfully uncomfortable. I kept running myself through every possible worst-case scenario, nearly wishing that it would all just go away, that I would not have to put so much of myself on the line. A few weeks later, the deal closed. *Thank God!*

I was able to face all of my fears by just sticking with it and facing everything head on. The fear impacting me had been concocted in my own head. I was able to build a successful business, four years and counting at the time of writing this book. This experience taught me the importance of telling myself only uplifting, positive, and true realities regarding my personal competency and capabilities. I am a fierce, young, successful business woman capable of anything I put my mind to, so I stopped telling myself: *I can't do it. I am not smart or aware enough.*

I started telling myself: *I can do anything.* I pushed myself to learn from new challenges. I would at least grow if things didn't work out exactly as planned, and I kept reminding myself that no matter what, I would figure things out.

What you tell yourself on a daily basis immensely affects who you will become. If you think you are a failure and that you are stupid, these things will manifest in your life. However, if you know and truly believe you are intelligent, capable, and talented, these positive things will be manifested into reality instead. That endless loop that keeps playing in your head (whether positive or negative) will significantly impact your life.

Some research shows that if you mull over the negative in your life, you will then feel worse, and you will feel less capable of solving your problems. You need to start your efforts with your own mind. You cannot allow self-doubt to sabotage your future or success. Dwelling on what you perceive to be your shortcomings will make them real to you. This variety of self-talk fuels every negative and non-empowering story that you feed to yourself until they become a self-fulfilling prophecy.

Apart from yourself, you also need to deal with the negativity around you. While self-control is already difficult, so is controlling or fixing the negative people around you. At one point or another, we have all been victims of people putting us down. Keep in mind that these people are quite commonplace, and equally mundane. Unfortunately, some of us still start believing it when people put us down enough.

You and only you have the power to choose what you will allow inside, what you focus on, and what will bother or affect you. Maintain your power to choose who and what to keep in your life. Here are some wise words from one of my favorite personal idols, Jim Rohn:

"Stand guard at the door of your mind."

I believe that this is a powerful way to see any given situation. Our thoughts shape everything that we do and see in reality, so you must exercise extra caution in what you allow to enter your mind. Remember that you always have a choice in this, regardless of what people say.

When times get tough, how will you deal with it? What can you do that will make it better? How could you make it worse? Will you sit and cry? Will you pull the covers over your head? Your reaction is your choice.

As a young female entrepreneur, I face battles with all kinds of negative people. As the proprietress of a gastro pub, I dealt with many rude customers whose comments were made in an attempt to bring me down. I calmly accepted these as plenty of people would walk into my gastro pub and say, "Oh, this must be your daddy's place," or "Oh, this is your husband's place, right?"

I used to get offended by their responses sometimes, because my father was not the owner. I am the owner, his daughter. My husband was not the owner. I am not even married. People failed to acknowledge that a young woman was strong enough and brave enough to do these things alone. They would not acknowledge that a woman had the resources and capabilities to do something like this; and to do it all on her own, absolutely killing it nonetheless!

"This is bullshit," one customer said. "A woman shouldn't be the owner of a bar. She shouldn't own anything. She shouldn't be the boss. It's not right." People have tried to degrade me countless times in my ventures as an entrepreneur, a real estate investor, and as a hospitality business owner.

I remember when I would walk through potential commercial properties I wanted to buy, and the vendors and selling agents would pay zero attention to me. I would go with my real estate agent or my uncle, and the vendors and agents would only speak with them because they did not think the purchase would be made by me. I started using this negativity as fuel rather than letting it leave me feeling disempowered.

There will be many times like this when people are essentially ignoring an aspect of you that they do not like. They may not like that you are successful, or that you have the potential or capabilities to do things well. If you want to get anywhere worth going to in this world, never allow these comments or remarks from others to pull you down or break your spirit. If you do, when opportunities in life present themselves, your brain might automatically start with:

"Oh my god, I cannot do this, I am not [smart, good, or worthy] enough."

If you start by telling yourself you cannot do something, soon enough you will not be able to. It will be just as you told yourself it would be: a self-fulfilling prophecy paralyzing you from taking action. You must immediately stop telling yourself any kind of limiting belief. Replace each of them with thoughts that serve you; with beliefs and concepts that will empower you.

Once you replace those negative thoughts, keep pushing through your fears and self-doubt. In moving forward, you will start seeing more opportunities to grow, and this is where the magic really happens. In entrepreneurism, as well as in business and investing, limiting beliefs in your mind are the biggest obstacle. <u>Failure is never an option.</u>

# 2. Abandoning Security

This obstacle stems from the stress and worry of an unsteady paycheck. There is something very comforting to most people about knowing exactly what is coming to them at the end of their next pay period. They feel secure in knowing for certain how much they should expect when payroll comes around, and it can be very scary to lose this.

The instability of being an entrepreneur is not necessarily for the faint of heart. When you are running your own business (be that in real estate or anything else), there is a component of risk and uncertainty in terms of how much you make at the end of the day. As an entrepreneur, you will be paid solely by your own productivity and success.

I mitigate this obstacle by putting 100% of my energy and effort into the business, or the real estate venture that I choose to take on. Like my grandparents, my philosophy is that failure will never be an option. I will find a solution or I will make a solution to be profitable no matter what happens along the way. How much I make is tied very closely to how much time and effort I put into my businesses.

Fear always sets in before every deal or investment, especially in the beginning stages of entrepreneurism and investing. However, the more deals and investments you make, the more experience and practice you will have, and the more your fear will slowly dissipate. You can deal with instability by:

A.   Taking Calculated Risks

- Ensure that you have enough knowledge in the industry that you are going into.
- Know which deal is good and why.
- Know a good business and how to evaluate it.
- Have awareness of the potential downsides and risks involved before jumping in.

In knowing all the possibilities and the outcomes that can happen, you will be better prepared. If you already have experience with closing a real estate deal, or if you have already opened a business or two, you will know what to expect or look for in the future. By knowing your best - and worst - case scenarios, you decrease your fear of the risks involved.

B.   Having Faith in Yourself.

Maintain confidence in your abilities in whatever business you go into. This will at the very least help you rest more assuredly, because you will know that you are fully capable of handling anything that might come your way. If you embrace an unwavering faith in yourself, in doing so, your mind will be put at ease from any unnecessary stress, worry, and sleepless nights.

# 3. Raising Capital

Finding ways to raise money or capital for starting a company, or buying real estate, can be very difficult sometimes. In Chapter Five, I will further detail available resources. For now, I want you to know that you will need to get creative instead of viewing it as a road block. Do not give up on your dreams. There are zero excuses when it comes to pursuing what you really want. In the beginning, you might need to learn how to cut back and bootstrap a little, but know that there is always a way. You may need to put yourself through many uncomfortable situations to find the funding you are looking for, but capital is available. Remember, there is a lot of money out there, and that money is accessible to everyone who wants it badly enough.

# 4. Maintaining Focus

Entrepreneurs are known for finding new ways of capitalizing, making more money, and finding new streams of income. While having such a variety of ideas can be fantastic, it can also become overwhelming. If you lack the focus to narrow down what exactly it is you are trying to do, your chances of success will remain marginal. You need to work on one thing at a time.

As an entrepreneur, your job is to zero in on your brightest ideas, and see everything through to the end. If you lack the focus required, then you will waste your time bouncing throughout hundreds of moving parts, and you will run the risk of not achieving anything. You will end up doing a hundred things at once, all the while getting nothing accomplished.

There are always so many things I want to do – plenty of new businesses to start, and new properties or ventures to take on. There were times when I found myself taking on too much all at once, and I felt overwhelmed with the resulting burden. There were so many things to do, and it all seemed bigger than it actually was because I didn't divide it into bite size chunks. I spread myself too thin, I was running around frantically, and because I felt so overwhelmed, I was unable to give each project my full attention.

Over the years, I learned to keep myself laser focused on any given task. I now maintain that focus until the task is at a place where I can step away. I practically automate one project before I move on to any other.

Without that 100% focus and dedication to your craft, task, or business, nothing will ever fully bloom. Giving only 50% of your attention will equal very little success in the long term. To harness 100% of your focus, you need to learn how to prioritize, to develop the ability to meticulously and effectively plan your day. This will ensure that you are making steady, consistent progress towards the goal at hand. Time management is key when it comes to getting laser focused.

# 5. *Managing People*

This obstacle is an art form in of itself. As an entrepreneur, you need to build and develop great teams of people around you, consistently motivate them, and keep everyone on track with your goals. This is not an easy task, but it needs to be done because you cannot do everything yourself. Staffing and managing people have always been the hardest tasks for me because there have been many times when I have been left disappointed. However, I learned that success will be found if you just keep rolling with this process. You have to keep adjusting, working at it, and spending time on it.

Staffing seems to be an ongoing issue for restaurant/bars. In the early days of running my gastro pub, I faced what appeared to be an insurmountable problem. On a particular Friday night (our busiest night of the week) we lost one staff member at the last minute, and not only that, another employee called in sick. We only had two people for dinner service and a live band event in the evening. We usually required at least up to six staff members on a Friday night, so because of the abrupt absences I had to personally jump in and work my butt off all night.

The sheer volume of customers made it feel near impossible when I first stepped into it, but my manager and I maintained our game faces, and we focused on our task until the end. We had no choice other than to move forward and get it done. Period. There was no other option. I served at the fastest pace of my barmaid career, and the customers were beyond demanding. They did not care that we were short staffed, and frankly that shouldn't have mattered to them either. I could have gotten completely flustered, surrendered to the night, called off the band, and shut the doors OR I could power through, remain positive, and get it done.

I chose to give it the best I possibly could, and not allow any of the customers or the lack of reliable staff to bring me down. We ended up crushing it. We kept at it until four in the morning, and the night turned out to be a huge success. When every customer cleared out, I felt really good and proud of myself. I felt this way not only because I handled each situation, but also because of how I was able to hold my focus above all the noise and negativity.

I was able to stand up against my own self-talk, and rock the show until the bitter end. I persevered, made the absolute best of my situation, and as a bonus, I profited well that night. However, staffing and managing people well will help you avoid having to face this kind of problem. When you face an obstacle like this, it is your responsibility to make the choice of creating a solution instead of caving in. Remember that attracting and keeping quality people on hand is one of the most important things in business, and an ongoing challenge. You need to remember to pick your teams wisely.

You should always trust your gut when it comes to impressions, and ensure that you take the time to nurture the relationships that you choose. Empower your team by providing incentives that matter to them on a personal level, and also by consistently making an effort to keep them motivated. If you do not do these things, you will find yourself working your butt off too regularly, and this will slow you down on your path to success.

# 6. Making Difficult Decisions

Being a visionary for your business can be stressful. As an entrepreneur you will have no superiors telling you:

- What to do
- How to solve a problem
- How to increase your sales

- What targets you need to hit each month
- How you can retain customers
- How to make more money

Everything is up to you, and it all falls on you to figure out a way through each storm and each difficult decision. You need to remain strong and confident, and you need to believe that you will find a solution. You are the only one who has your vision, the only one who can say whether or not any solution is the right path or the correct choice for your company. Again, the moment that you tell yourself that it is impossible for you to accomplish something, or that you are not good enough, that is when you start failing to solve any of your problems. You will end up getting in your own way, instead of seeing a solution or finding a way to succeed.

You need to train yourself to look for opportunities, instead of telling yourself that you are facing impossible odds because nobody is directing your life. Nobody will tell you how to be happy or successful, how to save money, or how and where to invest.

You will always have choices. In every single situation, remember that you always have at least three choices:

1. You can do nothing
2. You can take the path that is currently available
3. You can make your own path

It is important that you never see yourself as being at a dead end; this should never be the case. You need to be resourceful instead of admitting defeat. You need to be solution focused instead of problem oriented. If you see issues as challenges that require creative thought and resources, as opposed to dead ends or deal breakers, this mindset will get you much further in life.

When it comes to real estate, you are the only one who will decide whether or not you will renovate, invest, buy, or sell. You are the only one who decides how and what you will negotiate, which financing methods you will use, which tenants you want to live in your property, and so on. Nobody tells you what you should do; your business is solely dependent on your decisions, your direction and vision, so do not let self-doubt delay or stop you. You need to move ahead with your best decision at the time, and then shift accordingly as you go.

# Success Breeds Success

My pure will and my desire for financial wealth and freedom drive me to succeed through any circumstances that life throws my way. The more I succeed, the more I find myself wanting to grow, to build and create a life that I truly want on my terms. In my core, I know such a life is possible, and that I am capable of achieving my dreams. I refuse to believe or tell myself anything else.

Self-talk itself is one of the most important aspects of this section because if you stand in your own way towards achievement, towards what you really want to do, nothing will ever happen with your life. Let that sink in for a moment, because you need to understand that sometimes you stop yourself from achieving any kind of success.

I have now shared some of the main obstacles that entrepreneurs face, and I believe this will help you avoid any of them impacting suddenly as you approach your goals.

I am confident that you will accumulate the necessary tools to see the bottlenecks, to prepare for their arrival, and know how to overcome them. Yes, there will always be the unforeseen bumps in the road, and my advice for those is to expect the unexpected. Prepare yourself for the problems approaching you, deal with them as they come, and keep a confident stride as they arise no matter what. Know that when you wake up, you might receive five calls in the morning. There are many things that may have gone wrong that you need to fix.

There are many probable challenges and issues, some you have experienced and others have been shared with you. Expect that 3:00am call tomorrow, and become a problem solver. Do not be afraid of giving up a life of certainty and mediocrity to go for what you truly desire.

# Chapter Highlights

- Be mindful of your own self-talk.
- What you tell yourself on a daily basis immensely affects who you become and how successful you will be.
- Write down your limiting beliefs and what you tell yourself on a daily basis.
- I want you to see it in black and white and confront them now.
- Most of your fears and obstacles are internal/self-inflicted.
- Strengthen your resolve, calculate your risks, and have faith in yourself.
- You can leave the "security" of knowing what to expect from your paycheck every pay period.
- There are ways to get started with raising capital. These options will be explored in Chapter Five.
- To become laser focused, time management is key.
- When it comes to hiring staff and impressions, you need to trust your gut.
- Ensure that you take the time to nurture the relationships you choose.
- You need to be <u>solution focused.</u> Instead of problem oriented.
- Train yourself to look for opportunities in all things that come your way (good and bad).
- Break through your own fears and self-doubts.
- Stop telling yourself limiting beliefs.
- Replace them with beliefs and thoughts that will serve and empower you.

*Chapter 3*

# THE WEALTHY BARMAID PERSEVERES AGAINST ALL ODDS

The most important aspect of becoming successful is perseverance. Your sustained long-term effort is necessary to accomplish anything in life. No matter the pursuit, to arm your core with the virtue of perseverance is to nearly guarantee your success. People often rob themselves of their own success when they do not have the perseverance to see their goals through to the end.

As I mentioned briefly in the previous chapter, in order to develop perseverance in everyday life, you need to have faith. You need to believe that you can succeed and meet any goal set forth. An unwavering faith and strong belief in yourself ensures, as well as sustains, motivation while you continually strive towards your goals, regardless of the obstacles you might come up against.

On the other hand, if you do not have this belief in yourself, the likelihood is that you will quit. Quitting will never lead to success. It reinforces and substantiates your own theories presupposing that you would not have succeeded anyway. You will enter a cycle where you keep returning to those thoughts over and over again without making any progress. A mindset like this can quickly develop into a habit, and these habits sabotage any chance you have of meeting success.

Wealth begins with possessing the deep inner belief that you can succeed no matter what. It is then about maintaining that faith towards never giving up on your dreams. Equip yourself with the mindset that your success is just around the corner. There will be obstacles – some major ones – but with the belief of inevitable success, you will revise your game plans and tweak your strategies. Having faith in yourself dramatically improves your chances of success in the long term.

I consider myself a survivor. I know that no matter what happens to me in life, I will persevere. This mentality helps me along the path towards achievement, and I will not allow myself to give into defeat of any kind. If I make mistakes along the way, or suffer any temporary setbacks, I never settle until I reach my desired outcome. Over the course of adulthood and my career, I learned that my desired outcome is necessary in both life and business.

Focusing on your desired outcome is a mentality that you have to condition yourself to follow. How do you deal with setbacks? How do you deal with tough blows or unexpected events? How you handle these situations shapes your destiny more than when things actually go your way. This is where your true inner self will shine and where you will show the world (and more importantly show yourself) what you are really made of.

How you let these events influence your life and career is critical, because crisis can make or break you. The only reason that Oprah started hosting a TV show was because she failed as a news anchor. Someone actually told her that she was not fit for television. Richard Branson overcame dyslexia and in addition to founding the Virgin Group, he started over 400 companies. Steve Jobs was fired from his own company before he became a household name with Apple.

Milton Hershey started three different candy companies before The Hershey Company sold on shelves across the world. Stephen King's first novel was rejected thirty times before he got it published. Similarly, Jay-Z was unable to find a record label that would sign him, so he decided to start his own. Walt Disney was fired from a newspaper for lacking imagination, and having no original ideas.

These icons are all great examples of persevering because they never gave up on their dreams. They never stopped taking action or pursuing their goals, pushing through all obstacles arising in front of them. They pushed beyond anything that threatened to take away their dreams.

You need to rise above the noise and negativity, and release those who want to pull you down. Hold your dreams close, and keep them tightly in your grasp. Do not allow anyone to pry them from you, because you deserve a life that is designed purposefully by you and for you. Your life should become all that you ever dreamed it could be.

# *Always Improve Your Position*

My grandparents demonstrated a great level of perseverance. At any point in time they could have decided to pack everything up and return to Serbia, their home country, where they had a house, family, work, connections, and community. Going back home was always an option for them when things got too tough. Many migrant families who ventured to North America eventually realized that they did not like it, or that it wasn't for them and it was not uncommon for some to move back after a few years. While North America has been known to be a land of opportunity, it is also a very difficult place. If you do not have the right mindset and work ethic for success, it can be a very scary and harsh environment.

My grandparents nearly lost their shirts numerous times in their ventures. I remember when they had tenants who did not pay rent for six months during a time when my grandparents were barely earning enough for their mortgage payments. However, they struggled through it and moved their money around, figuring it out until they were able to find better tenants.

Could my grandparents have sold the rental, and quit investing in real estate because of that bad experience? Absolutely, but they didn't. They would never and will never allow themselves to be held back from the notion that owning real estate is an important part of building success in this country.

When they were running their largest restaurant/bar (their biggest piece of property at the time) they nearly declared bankruptcy. Everything they had was on the line, and everything could have been taken away. While this was one of their scariest moments, even though they were over-leveraged, they worked day and night to come up with a solution to the problem. They found one after a few months, and they were able to restore everything and finally breathe again.

My grandparents found the help they needed and then they were able to turn it all around. During that time, not once did they think of giving up or taking the easy way out. Over the course of their life (from their first move to Canada through building up their wealth) they trained themselves to stick with whatever they were doing, pushing themselves forward in whatever they started or believed in. They were committed to making things happen even when the odds were against them.

For me, this is the moral of their story:

- Dedication
- Determination
- Drive

Their dreams were worth more than the pain they were temporarily experiencing during any rough times. Through their hard work, and massive efforts to be where they are today, they never gave up. At no point did they question why they believed they could accomplish it; they just knew that they could. Their drive reminds me of the words of Winston Churchill:

"If you are going through hell, keep going."

My grandparents maintained the belief that they were capable. They are the epitome of Churchill's assertion, and a great example of succeeding against all odds. I keep their dedication, determination, and drive close to heart when I need to persevere through the rough times of my life.

# *Just Keep Swimming*

When I was a recent MBA graduate with a good amount of experience under my belt, I decided that I wanted new experiences. I opted to move to a new city with new surroundings. In search of opportunity and a fresh environment, I packed all my things and headed to Toronto.

My bartending and hospitality management experience continued and my confidence had grown as I managed a staff of 20 – at the age of eighteen. I had also gained marketing and advertising experience from my jewelry and accessories boutique, while holding an account manager position with a boutique advertising agency for almost two years. Feeling that I now possessed many skills needed to make my mark in the world, my plan was to share my experience and work ethics with a great company. However, this did not go as well as I planned it. When I graduated with my MBA, the job market had completely changed. The country was in mid-recession.

Jeff Muzzerall (Director of the Corporate Connections Centre at the Rotman School of Management, University of Toronto) described the crisis of 2008 for young graduates:

If you were entering your MBA in 2006 at peak employment, you were looking at a 94% placement rate within three months of graduating. But if you are graduating in 2008, into the greatest depression since the First World War, and expecting similar results, [then] that was not going to happen.

Needless to say, jobs were not plentiful and because of the tough job market, I was almost unemployable even with the experience I gained while I was earning my degrees. I decided to make it my full-time job to find work in my field, and I applied countless times. I did all the right things, but still nothing ended up catching. Most companies hiring at the time were doing so from within. Each of them did their best to keep up employee morale during that difficult period. Instead of giving up and going back to my hometown empty handed, I started getting creative.

I designed my own campaign, and I made it my mission to land a job in my field and to earn some valuable experience. I had a t-shirt made up with huge neon pink lettering with "Hire Me" on the front, and "MBA Marketing" on the back. I wore this shirt all around town for weeks. I had a few interviews lined up shortly after, and a few offers for small contract jobs, but nothing matched my education or my experience. It was difficult hearing 'no' after 'no', getting rejected by companies over and over again; especially the ones I was particularly interested in.

I didn't let it get me down. I kept wearing the shirt and networking as much as I possibly could. I still applied in person, door to door, and online. I just kept swimming. After two months of this particular effort, I found an opportunity when I was at a launch party for a new fragrance. I was networking and mingling with the crowd, and my friend brought me into a conversation. They introduced me to the owner of a public relations firm in Toronto who was handling the event. The owner took a shine to me while we chatted, and by the end of the night they asked me to join their team.

Starting the following Monday, I was in downtown Toronto, and I was doing something that I loved. I kept moving forward regardless of the rejections, the time taken, and the energy and effort required. For the entire time I was in Toronto, I also kept a bartending job because it was an expensive city to live in, and I was so used to working in that industry. This job also helped me save more money for future investments.

At the end of my efforts in Toronto, everything I went through paid off. If you do not give up going after what you really want, and you never allow defeat to be an option, it really does pay off. It is inevitable that you will succeed if you maintain a mindset of perseverance.

# *The Wealthy Barmaid Rolls with the Punches*

During the early days of running my gastro pub, I had so many restless nights as major stress, anxiety, and worries took over me. I was regularly there until three or four in the morning dealing with:

- Nasty drunk fights
- The police
- Vandalized property
- Toxic staff members
- Angry customers
- Theft
- Repairs that could have drowned me

My worries were especially high during slow seasons. *This is not what I want to be doing,* I thought to myself many times. *This is rough.* However, I kept at it until I figured out the important details of the business, and I learned how to control these issues. I knew that there was a way, and I knew it did not have to be so hard.

The last thing you want to hear as a business owner is that you need to do a major repair on your facility during your slowest season. Well, I heard it and was immediately horrified. Even though the business had been growing steadily since my acquisition, as I headed into a brutally slow summer season with a repair-induced cash-flow crisis looming in the shadows, I feared that this may spell the end of my business. As I started panicking about my bills, with no clear idea of what to do I remember saying to myself, *This is no fun. I don't need this. I am twenty-seven years old! I should not be making myself sick with worry!*

I had so much responsibility on my back, so I called my grand-father for advice. I was hoping he could make me feel better, and luckily he did. His voice was reassuring to me, deep and strong, and as we spoke about business, he was direct and loud. He mellowed his voice though, when he told me:

> Everything in life goes up and down, especially in business. It can never be a straight line, and it can't always go up. You have to prepare yourself for the lows, for the unforeseen bumps in the road.

> Especially in hospitality, it fluctuates greatly from season to season. You need to come up with things that make the slow seasons better, to get through it. And you need to always know that it will turn around.* Things will always turn around."

> * My grandfather and I have a disclaimer here:
> This is true if you are doing everything you can to continuously build and grow your business.

At that time, I started investing more in sponsoring sports teams during those slow seasons, and I put more effort into marketing and branding. I was bettering my business in all areas from the quality of service, more impressive food offerings and presentation, to more specials, promotions, and events. I would work day and night, coming up with things that would expand my business and drive more customers through the door.

My hard work paid off. No matter how difficult it was for me to keep going through the slow seasons, I pulled through. I had faith that my business would succeed no matter the season, and no matter the stress that my staff or any of my customers brought my way. I could have settled for a comfortable job. I could have cashed in, sold my businesses and rental properties, and dropped all responsibilities overnight.

It would have been so easy for me to give up during those sleepless nights, but I wouldn't have even one tenth of what I have today. My future would not look as bright as it does from where I stand now. I will never give up on my dreams, no matter what it takes.

# The Wealthy Barmaid Settles for Nothing Less Than Great

My hope for you is that you will find the same attitude to make it big and live financially free as I have from my experiences. Remember, success belongs to those who are willing to make sacrifices and work hard toward their goals, regardless of what happens. No matter the obstacles, you need to work through them and never give up. Fight through the hard days to earn the best days. Whenever you are stuck, or you spend too much time in your comfort zone without much progress, refer to the words of a personal idol of mine (one of the greats), John D. Rockefeller:

"Do not be afraid to give up the good to go for the great."

I keep this quote on me at all times. It is a positive reminder of opportunity whenever I need to step up and burst through any stagnancy, problems, or obstacles that I might be experiencing. When I think about going for the great, any situation of uncertainty and difficulty are actually blessings in disguise. Those rough times can be an opportunity if you allow your mind to be open to them and to see possibilities. They can take you to a whole new level if you are willing to accept the challenge.

The main ingredient here is also the unrelenting desire to succeed. If you quit while working towards something that you really want, you may never know how close you were to actualizing your dreams. The truth is that it is usually right after that point, when things get too hard and you want to give up, that success is right around the corner.

# *Chapter Highlights*

- For success, you need to maintain an unwavering faith and strong belief in yourself.
- Always improve your position.
- Keep moving forward, especially during difficult times.
- Perseverance is critical to success.
- How you deal with setbacks, tough blows, and unexpected events shapes your destiny.
- These rough times are actually opportunities.
- Overcome feelings of defeat, stress, anxiety with unrelenting persistence and you will see places beyond your expectations.

*Chapter 4*

# THE WEALTHY BARMAID PASSIONATELY INVESTS IN REAL ESTATE

After my grandparents had been working together at their first restaurant/bar for eleven successful years, cashflow was increasing. Through those years, they had persistently saved money from their business and invested it right back into additional rental properties. Their empire grew little by little, and their income was great, which was very affirming. Together they accomplished my grandfather's dream of owning a successful business as well as a growing real estate portfolio. In short, their strategies worked.

After those eleven years, my grandfather had his sights set on something bigger: another restaurant/bar on a much more predominant street in Niagara Falls. Again he found himself facing a huge risk, but he knew that it would be worth it for a better future, so he did it. He put their first business and commercial property up for sale. He took all their savings, sold the business, and made a deal with their bank. Before his family knew it, they owned a much larger, much more significant piece of prime real estate, which later proved to be their gold mine, and their golden ticket. However, this particular business was suffering greatly when they arrived.

There was a lot of family effort at that point because both my uncle and my mother were old enough to help. While my mother was finishing college, she helped my grandmother in the kitchen, prepping for meals and cooking, and she would also tend the bar. She and my uncle were instrumental in building the family business. My uncle pitched in wherever he could and was always keen to run a promotion to help increase exposure and sales.

My uncle, obviously cut from the same stone as my grandparents, had bigger plans for the establishment. So in my mother's last year of college, my uncle paid for a full vacation for my grandparents. Generous? Yes. Altruistic? Not so much. My uncle used the trip as a distraction so that he could do an entire renovation of the restaurant/bar while my grandparents were away. My uncle renovated the property, gutting it entirely while they were gone. They were so happy when they got back and saw the amazing transformation.

They continually worked diligently every day (and night) together, growing the business month after month. Nearly a year later, during their best month-to-date in 1986, my uncle suggested selling as business fluctuates greatly in the restaurant industry. After much debate, he convinced my grandparents to sell and then use the proceeds to buy an even bigger, more profitable business and commercial property in a nearby city. The strategies were already in place. My grandparents had already shown proof of concept with their first two businesses. This was repeatable. Over and over again. So, just as they had done previously, they turned this newly acquired business and property into an even more profitable model and when the time was right, they once again sold. They sold their second business for $1M, which would be like making $2.2M on a sale in today's economy! This was a big deal for my family as we remembered the lessons of my grandparents. We remembered the story of the $69.

Their new business was a restaurant/bar and also a nightclub. Always looking to differentiate and add value, my uncle and grandparents thought they could generate even more profits from unused square footage on the property. In a flash of genius, they turned the upstairs area into a dinner theater – often hosting Broadway performers and reputable, touring acts.

On the personal front, my grandparents also bought a house in what is still a very affluent neighborhood in Niagara Falls, Ontario. This was a turning point for them. My grandfather remembered his aspirations when they left Serbia with only $69 and no security whatsoever, and now here he was in the late '80s, after years of hard work. He and his family had more than he could ever have dreamed possible. They were now living in a neighborhood with doctors and lawyers in North America. They could afford cars and vacations, which was a long time coming. These strategies enabled my grandparents to far surpass their earlier goals of merely securing a more stable future for themselves and future generations.

# *The Wealthy Barmaid's First House*

I was very lucky to grow up around a family who always invested in real estate. I was able to see firsthand what it was all about, and what the results would be over time. To me, there was nothing *that* scary about investing in real estate. This is not to say that I necessarily knew every single detail about buying, owning, and maintaining properties. However, because I had seen so many people doing it around me, I knew more or less what was involved.

At the very least, I knew some of the risks going into it for myself. I also knew how much control I would have over my investment, and this part I liked a lot. Aside from a market completely crashing overnight, I was able to control everything else:

- How much I pay to purchase
- How much I put in for renovations
- Which tenants I keep
- Which tenants I get rid of
- How much to charge for rent
- When to sell the property
- How much to sell the property for

I was further ahead than most of my peers or people my age, unbeknownst to me at the time, because of my upbringing. My father encouraged me to buy my first piece of real estate when I was twenty-two, and then rent it out. I had enough money saved at that point, and he knew that it would be better spent on a mortgage down payment than on anything else.

I began a search for my first single-family unit. I researched at least a couple hundred properties before I selected the ones that I would walk through. After a few months of searching I found one that I liked because it met all my criteria. It was a two-story house, with three bedrooms upstairs and one bathroom. The family had been living there for generations, and they never did any work on it, so everything inside was extremely dated. All three bedrooms were tiny, the walls were very closed off, and the wallpaper was peeling. While I did see that it required a lot of work, I could also see that so much could be done to really open up the place. As an added bonus, the house was in a great neighborhood that held my attention.

I made an offer after my walkthrough. The asking price was a very good deal because the sellers were motivated to sell quickly. I drafted my offer at $7,000 less than their asking price, and I communicated that everything would be conditional upon acceptable financing and a satisfactory home inspection. My real estate agent called me later that evening to let me know that my offer had been accepted. I was sixty days away from owning my first house!

I then secured financing through a conventional bank with a traditional mortgage; a local credit union that was offering good rates at the time. I have strong relationships with them to this day for my financing needs. I remember my first time being in a room with the mortgage broker. I did not understand most of the details and terms she was telling me regarding my mortgage, so when I got home I read everything in full detail, trying my best to understand what it all meant.

My lack of knowledge (of the little details and the fine print) was the only area of the process that made me a little uncomfortable. My preference is to go into everything I do with a full understanding, but in this case I just kept moving forward. I knew the result that I was after, and I kept the big picture in mind. I kept learning what I needed as I went along, just like my grandparents did.

I locked myself into a fixed rate for five years because the offered rate was exceptional. I also knew that I would not be doing anything fancy with the mortgage over that time period. After taking care of the mortgage, I secured insurance for the house and ordered the home inspection. Everything went well and on schedule, and structurally there were no major issues with the house, so I felt confident waiving that condition.

Before I knew it, the sixty days passed and I owned my first property! My first real estate deal was such an exciting and proud moment for me. I will always remember that experience that would later lead to the development of a full-blown real estate empire.

When I showed my family the house, they instantly had visions of its potential – graciously sharing all their ideas. There was a sun room that had zero insulation that needed to be addressed (we have very cold winters in Canada). I also envisioned breaking down some of the walls to open up the space. While I was living in the property for a year, I steadily made minor renovations and within only two months of trying, I rented it out to my first tenants.

I soon realized that my earning potential was limited as I could only charge so much rent for an aesthetically very dated home. I decided that I needed to do more and by renovating, I would then be much more likely to find long-term renters, and my ROI would be much higher. I started with cleaning up the exterior of the property with quick fixes like buying a beautiful new mailbox and address numbers and painting the front porch. I then redid all the drywall and all of the ceilings. I installed new light fixtures throughout the house, and I even added some recessed ones to the sunroom.

I also installed new windows, doors and doorknobs – all furnishings consistent with a very contemporary style. In the kitchen, I redid the tiling, countertops, and I installed all-new cabinetry. I added an island in there as well, which was something I always looked forward to having. I knocked a wall out in order to open it up to the kitchen as well as the sunroom. I knocked another down in the kitchen, opening it up to the dining room and living room area. All of a sudden, I was standing in a very fresh, modern, open-concept property.

I retiled the bathroom too, including the entire shower, and I bought a brand-new bathtub. I spent countless hours on my hands and knees pulling up the original flooring, and I spent weeks getting the wallpaper off the wall. As the home came together, it was very obvious that none of it had been touched in at least seventy years. The baseboards, the light switches, everything was old. When the flooring was up I chose nice hardwood floors as an upgrade – but looking back, I would advise that vinyl or pre-finished laminates would have been a better decision due to durability for a rental.

Regardless, this house is my prized possession, and I still own it today. Honestly, it will always be my favorite property, and I have kept it rented out ever since. At the time, I was only thinking about the fact that one day (when I choose to retire and the mortgage is completely paid off) I would be able to live off the rental payments. My mindset from the start was future security, to pay it off while letting it appreciate over the course of my working life. My thought was that this first house would become my income when I retire, either by continuing to rent it out, or by selling it and living off the profits.

With how unsure and shaky the economy has been for the last couple decades (particularly the global economic recession of 2008), I learned there is no such thing as job security, safety, or retirement when it comes to either government or company pensions. At a young age, I was prompted by these conditions to decide and act upon taking my future into my own hands; to create my own security and pension plan. In the last seven years, I have become much savvier in the process. I currently enjoy a surplus of monthly income not only from that first house, but also from every subsequent house/rental property that I acquired since – not to mention the equity that has built up since then.

# Why the Wealthy Barmaid Loves Investing in Real Estate

At twenty-two, I did not know much about real estate at all. I did not go to school for it, nor did I study it day and night before making my first purchase. I was armed only with the facts inherited from my youth, watching many trusted family members invest in property through my childhood and onward. Because of this, I knew that it was the right decision and that my future self would thank me for it. I learned that real estate is a smart decision because I saw that it would pay off in some fashion later on down the road.

After my first investment, I was particularly set on single-family houses as I continued purchasing rental properties. After four years of focusing on those, I then felt ready to purchase my first commercial property, where I started my gastro pub. It was a huge step for me, not only in terms of business and income, but also for my net worth. My business operates from this property today, and it is nearly triple its original value. With this in mind, commercial real estate can be an extraordinary investment opportunity for many reasons which I will cover shortly.

Since I was twenty-two, I have been constantly amazed at the seemingly endless benefits from investing in real estate, and how it can provide a life of financial success and freedom:

1. It is not only the safest investment along with gold, but it also provides the best Return on Investment (ROI).
2. Historically speaking, its values have only gone up when considering all factors such as good location, the type of property, and quality of the building.
3. Over the long term, it provides and optimizes cashflow from rental income.
4. Its values are constantly appreciating, making it the type of investment that makes money while you sleep.
5. It can be used as a retirement plan by either cashing in when you sell, or by living off the cashflow from rental income.
6. It has the added bonus of hedging against inflation.

Remember, real estate is not terribly complex and you do not need a ton of education to succeed. By following my strategies for income-property investing you can quickly master this process which as illustrated earlier, is repeatable. As a major part of your portfolio, building wealth via real estate requires one thing: When you buy a property, hold it until you can make a substantial profit. Moreover, houses are neither ultra-complicated nor scary. There is tremendous comfort knowing that a house's performance is predictable. They produce income when rented, and house rents have a history of increasing.

Likewise, housing prices have increased at an average annual rate of roughly 5% for about as long as we can measure. During some years, houses go up in value at a much higher rate. Occasionally, they do not go up at all, and they can even drop in price. There are many houses that rarely drop in price, and those are the ones you want to buy. These are the qualities that I suggest you look for when purchasing real estate to ensure that its value will appreciate:

• A solid structure
• An advantageous location*

- Good price/deal
- An ordinary number of repairs

* You should study price trends around the location and see if house prices are accelerating faster in one area than in others. Check then to see if the average home price is more than in neighboring towns, because this will provide an idea of where the biggest demand is currently. Over time, you will develop a sense for which property prices are "fair" and which ones are overpriced. Usually, the best position is buying homes in newer, up-and-coming, trendy neighborhoods.

# *Residential versus Commercial Real Estate*

Houses are a unique investment because you can rent them out to provide income, but their value does not depend on that income. Even an empty house can make you money because it will appreciate as much as a full one. The value of other real estate options like multifamily homes (apartments) and commercial property (office buildings, strip malls, restaurants, and shops) depends on the income they produce, along with the building/structure itself. In regards to multifamily homes, if you rent an apartment or office space for below-market rent, it will be worth less money, whereas (once again) an empty house is worth just as much as a full one. Houses are much safer investments for a few reasons:

1. Less money is involved.
   - You can often buy a house with a smaller down payment and less risk.
   - Lenders routinely lend more against a house than any other type of property.

2. Houses have more buyers than commercial properties.
   - If you need to sell in a hurry, you always can – if you offer a house at a good price.
3. Houses rent faster and have fewer vacancies.
   - Apartment vacancies often run 10% to 20%.
   - House vacancies rarely exceed 5%.
   - Commercial properties can sit empty for months and even years at a time between tenants.
   - You need a lot of cash in the bank to survive a long-term vacancy in a larger building.

When you are buying a house, you typically deal with a homeowner who is in a hurry to sell. If a homeowner had plenty of time to sell, then they would wait for a retail price. When you decide to sell any real estate in a hurry, you will have to discount the price to sell it quickly. Learn this lesson:

Never put yourself in a position where
you have to sell in a hurry!

When you buy commercial (such as a multi-unit apartment property), you are buying from another investor. You still might be able to negotiate a good deal, but often you are dealing with someone who has more experience negotiating, and they might be better at it than you are. However, when you buy from a homeowner, you might have more negotiation experience, and therefore an advantage. You should never buy unless you can make a good deal.

When you sell a house, a buyer can usually get a loan for nearly the entire purchase price, and in some cases this will be for more money than what the buyer is actually paying. You as the seller will receive that entirely in cash on closing. With options such as Seller Financing, also known as Vendor Take Back (VTB), you have the option of financing the sale for the buyer to generate interest income, which is available if the buyer cannot secure a loan from a bank. Buyers who need help with financing beyond conventional lenders are not uncommon. Often, if you agree to a VTB then you can sell at an even higher price, which will be explored more in Chapter Six.

Commercial properties require more money up front than residential properties, which means there are fewer potential buyers. One potential disadvantage of selling an apartment building or commercial property is the negotiation. The typical buyer will be an investor, and they will negotiate to get the best price and terms that they can. In contrast, when investing in several houses (rather than multifamily homes or a commercial property), a major advantage is your ability to diversify by investing in different price ranges. You can own less expensive and more expensive houses all at once. Diversifying your investment this way will give you the safety of the lower-priced properties that rarely drop in value, and the upside potential of the higher-priced ones that jump more in price during a boom.

I am not advising against purchasing apartment buildings or multi-unit commercial properties. However, if you are a novice investor, I would suggest that you first gain some experience with residential income properties. My advice is for you to <u>choose one investing strategy</u> and <u>master it before moving on to another</u>. It really is very easy to get distracted by "shiny object syndrome" and then lose your focus, but you need to remember not to give into the temptation of dabbling in a whole bunch of different strategies when you are just getting started.

Personally, I did multiple deals involving single-family homes before I ventured into commercial properties. When you are ready, certain advantages come with the purchase of commercial property, one of the biggest being that the assets are generally secured by leases. These provide a regular income stream, which is significantly higher than typical stock dividend yields, or rental income from an average residential house.

While residential leases are usually for shorter term periods, it is not uncommon for some commercial real estate leases to last ten years or more; they are usually at the very least one year long. This long-term span of rent gives the commercial real estate holder a considerable amount of cashflow stability when the building is occupied by long-term tenants. In areas where the amount of new construction is either limited by land or law, commercial real estate can have impressive returns and considerable monthly cashflow. Rental rates with commercial properties are calculated per square foot.

Depending on where you are, this could be anywhere from $12/sq ft in less populated urban areas, to $4,500/sq ft in places like downtown Hong Kong, where further development is nearly impossible. Triple net leases are the most common with commercial real estate properties. The concept here is that generally, you as the property owner do not have to pay any expenses on the property, such as property taxes and utilities. The lessee handles all property expenses directly.

Overall, the best reason to invest in commercial properties is their excellent appreciation/earning potential. Appreciation, more than any other factor, provides tremendous growth opportunity for your net worth. Generally, the annual return for commercial properties is between 6% and 12% of the purchase price depending on the area. This is a much higher range than what typically exists for single-family-home properties; roughly 5%, as we will cover next.

Let's say you invested $125,000 into a $500,000 commercial property; that would be a 25% down payment. It is not inconceivable for someone to offer you $750,000 or more after three years to buy it. If your mortgage was amortized over fifteen years, you will have then paid it down roughly $134,705. Add that to the $250,000 capital gain ($750,000 to $500,000) and you will have now turned your initial investment of $125,000 into $384,705. This is a 33% return in three years! This result would mean that you made $259,705 after only three years! Even after your recaptured depreciation tax, this is pretty impressive, is it not?

Many investors, rather than selling, will remortgage their property, which is also known as refinancing. They will pull out some equity and repeat the process. In most cases, rental income should increase enough over time to cover the additional mortgage amount. While there are many advantageous reasons to invest in commercial real estate over residential, there are also some challenges to consider:

1.  Bigger initial investment. Acquiring a commercial property typically requires more capital up front than a residential property will; a 25% to 50% down payment is the norm. The higher costs to 'getting in the game' come in the form of not only a higher down payment but also:

- Closing costs
- Legal fees
- Environmental assessments
- Phase I and sometimes Phase II environmental studies on the property
- Appraisals
- Land transfer taxes
- Property inspections
- Bank fees and mortgage commissions
- Title insurance

- Incorporation costs
- Legal disbursements
- Zoning reports
- City tax certificates
- Engineering reports
- Registry office searches
- Utility searches
- Deed registration
- Corporate searches
- Fire
- Electrical
- Surveys
- Repairs
- Miscellaneous Capital Expenditures

These costs can reach a total of thousands of dollars, and with larger buildings, they can be hundreds of thousands.

- There is also the high risk of vacancy with commercial properties
- It often takes much longer to fill a commercial unit than a residential one
- You will need a lot of money in the bank to weather the storm (potentially months) of having a vacant unit during down economies

2.  Time commitment. An example: if you own a commercial retail building with five tenants, or even just a few, you have more to manage than you do with a residential investment. With commercial, you are likely dealing with:

    •   Multiple leases
    •   Annual Common Area Maintenance (CAM) adjustments
    •   Costs that tenants are responsible for
    •   Miscellaneous maintenance issues
    •   Public safety concerns
    •   Overall, you have more to manage and this requires more time on your part. You could hire a property management company but they can charge between 5-10% of rent revenue for their services. Services include lease administration. If you choose to do it yourself, these factors will require more of a time investment as well as financial

3.  Professional help is required as well as more active property management. Unless you are licensed to do so, you will need to hire someone for:

    •   Maintenance
    •   Emergencies
    •   Repair issues
    •   This added cost is not ideal, but you will need to add it to your list of expenses in order to properly care for your property

4.   More risk:

- Properties intended for commercial use have more public visitors
- More people on the property each day can get hurt or do something to damage your property
- Cars can hit patrons in parking lots
- People can slip on ice during the winter
- Vandals can spray paint the sides of the building
- Unfortunately, I have experienced all the above over the years. Including those who invent stories of injury, and are just trying to cash in from a lawsuit. This is why you must be diligent about your insurance coverage, as well as ensuring that you have the best lawyers. These risks are the costs for a higher reward. You need to make sure that you have extensive insurance coverage for all the liabilities that come with owning commercial property

Investing in commercial properties is a higher risk, higher reward type of real estate investment, and it appeals to more sophisticated investors looking for a challenge. If you do not have the capital to invest in commercial properties, but you still want the challenge, you do have another option: Real Estate Investment Trusts (REITs). This option offers small-scale investors a chance to enjoy the profits found in commercial investing without most of the risk, time, energy, and effort. Managers of REITs handle the details of the purchase (maintenance, tenants, and so on), and an investor buys a share of the REIT just like a stock. REITs are also more liquid than actually owning a commercial property.

# As Little As 5% a Year Appreciation Can Make a Barmaid Wealthy

As mentioned above, research shows that real estate increases in value of about 6.1 % a year according to the US Census Bureau, but for this example, I will use a very conservative estimate of 5%. If you buy a property that will produce income, your return will be much higher than 5%. If you borrow most of your purchase price, your rate of return could be 25% or more!

Suppose you bought a house at a retail price of $120,000. If you borrowed 80% of your purchase price, then you would need a 20% ($24,000) down payment. If the rental income covers your monthly payments and the house appreciated at 5% the following year, 5% of $120,000 is $6,000. This would be a 25% return on your $24,000 investment!

If you learn how to buy property at below-market prices, and finance even more of the purchase price, your rate of return increases considerably. The power in buying real estate on leverage takes shape in the following years as your profits and equity increase at a compounded rate. Your property value increases annually and all the while you are paying down your debt, and eventually paying it off entirely (See Figure 1). No other investment, not even stocks, can provide such a reliable ROI.

Do you know how long it takes an investment to double in value if it goes up 5% each year? The answer can be calculated by using the rule of 72. You can calculate how long it will take to double your money by dividing the compounded rate of return into the number 72.

# Leverage with Real Estate Investments Builds your Wealth

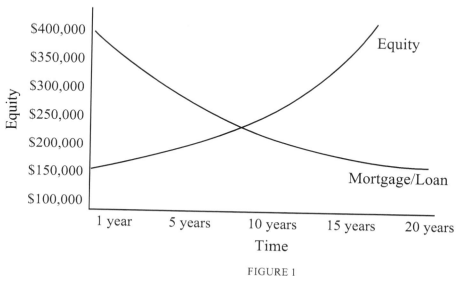

FIGURE 1

Let me illustrate this for you. If you take the interest you would earn from a savings account at a bank (in this example 5%) and divide that into 72, you will get 14.4. This means that at a rate of 5% a year, it will take 14.4 years for a house to double in value. Considering your initial investment, and the idea that your money will increase while you sleep, this is also pretty impressive, is it not?

# Real Estate as Retirement Income

I love investing in real estate for retirement purposes. Again, when I was buying my first house at the age of twenty-two, my thought process was to secure cashflow for whenever I choose to retire. I want to avoid being in a desperate or weak position, so my priority has been to set myself up in such a way that I can survive once I am no longer working. The way I did this also applies in case something ever goes wrong and I cannot physically work. Retirement and security is why I started investing in passive income strategies such as investment properties.

The goal as you approach retirement is to optimize the cashflow from each property. This is done by lowering, or even eliminating your mortgage, which gives you more money to live off of each month. Over the years, as your property is appreciating and building up equity, you will also be able to refinance it (if need be) to use a sizeable portion of the equity for whatever purpose needed. You can also sell and cash it all in for retirement if you so choose. However, if you sell, you need to ensure that you have enough money to last you a certain amount of time.

How many people do you know who are working at a job they don't like, for more than half their lifetime, just to get the retirement benefits? Today this strategy is a very risky one as many companies have been unable to fulfill any obligation to long-term employees. For some of them it was due to bankruptcy, while for others they were actually underfunding their retirement plans. As mentioned before, I will never look to any company or the government to provide security or be my safeguard.

Real estate can be a growing source of income, and a bonus benefit is that this income also protects you from inflation. The federal government has the ability to stimulate economic activity by increasing the amount of money we all have. They do this both by adding to the amount of money in circulation, as well as the amount of money the government lends to banks at relatively low interest rates. The banks, in turn, can lend this money to consumers and businesses, thereby stimulating more purchasing. Inflation drives the prices of all commodities up, including land and real estate prices.

Investing in real estate protects you against inflation because both your house and your rent prices will keep up with inflation increases. Research shows real estate is rising in value about 6.1 % a year, outpacing inflation by an average of 33% annually (US Census Bureau). A well-leveraged house allows you to make a dramatic profit.

During inflationary times, investing in assets such as real estate will protect you from tremendous loss in the purchasing power that inflation causes. When you are a real estate investor, you will not have to fear or hate inflation. It will take far less time for you to generate enough income by investing in a few houses than it will if you work twenty years for a company to cash in on their retirement plan. If we are being honest, it is highly unlikely that the end result with a company retirement plan will be sufficient enough to survive on anyway. Here are a couple more advantages of real estate to keep in mind:

1. The money that you borrow against a house is tax-free.
2. Houses make good collateral for loans.
3. The money you pull out of your equity through a refinance is also tax-free.

When you buy and hold a house for some time, as real estate values increase, the value of your property will double at some point. The average time for property in my area to double in value is roughly eight years. In larger, more metropolitan cities, and growing urban areas, this time frame is much shorter. Once a house has doubled in value, while the loan has been simultaneously paid down significantly, an investor with good credit in a good credit market can typically borrow 80% of the appraised value.

The more rental properties you own, the more cashflow and equity will then be available to you for whatever you choose to do with it in the future. Ideally, you will use refinancing to invest in more real estate!

# *Real Estate is Awesome…Seriously*

First and foremost, real estate provides housing for people. It can be used to build equity and grow your net worth, while producing a livable monthly cashflow. Real estate can be a retirement plan, either by selling it and cashing in, or living off the cashflow provided by the tenants paying you rent. Real estate can also be used as collateral to secure other loans – which is invaluable both for emergencies, or for expanding your real estate empire. Real estate can also provide funding through refinancing, pulling out your equity in the form of cash or lines of credit to be used for some other investing purposes.

I absolutely love investing in real estate, if you could not tell. As I mentioned, one of my favorite aspects of investing in real estate is that it is one of the only investments where you have the most control. These aspects are entirely up to you:

- How and when you will purchase the property
- Your final purchase price
- Negotiations are more flexible as you gain more experience
- What financing strategy to use (see Chapter 5)
- What to upgrade or renovate
- And to what degree
- How to manage it
- When to sell
- How high you will set the price
- What terms you will agree to

It definitely makes my future look brighter, and I want you to have these tools to make your future look brighter too. Real estate is remarkably accessible to investors. Not only is it easy to understand and easy to find, but more significantly, it is easy to finance. In addition to many of the traditional ways of financing properties, there are many sources of private/owner financing strategies and options available. There are also real estate financing options for every type of property. There is a selection for almost every type of buyer, including:

- Low income to no income
- Poor credit to no credit
- Little down to nothing down
- Experience to no experience

There are no insurmountable financial barriers to your entry. The main reason for this is that real estate provides significant insurable collateral for any mortgage no matter who the lender might be. When loans are secured against real estate, lenders feel more "secure." Real estate is appreciable, increasing in value over time, and every type of lender enjoys this fact. Also, real estate is extremely leverageable.

The truth is that wealth is built by taking on debt. Consider the fact that it's not very common for someone to pay all cash for a home or any other real estate investment. In reality, many finance most of the price (if not all of it) through a mortgage. They will then get the unbelievable benefit of receiving appreciation on the entire value of the property, not just on the value of what they put in with their down payment. They receive this benefit while only having to initially invest a small portion of the purchase price.

As outlined above, even if the market goes up by 5%, you would end up with a 25% ROI (if you put down a 20% down payment). This illustrates one of the most important aspects of real estate: it is leveraged. Once you have built up an equity position through an investment property, you can leverage that investment for cash in one of two ways:

Secure a second loan against the increased equity.

OR

Refinance the original loan amount plus the increase in equity.

# Additional Benefits
# of Real Estate Investing

When you look at your net investment and the return on that, real estate is far above any other investment; again, including the stock market. Another major bonus of real estate is cashflow, as people are paying down your mortgage when renting your home. In exchange for a place to live, your tenants will build up your equity. If you buy the property correctly, they provide you with the opportunity to get unearned income in the form of positive cashflow. This is a three-way win for you: You get appreciation, debt pay-down, and positive cashflow.

Another unique and attractive advantage to real estate is that it is improvable. You can force appreciation through restorations and renovations. Real estate is a tangible asset (it is made of wood, concrete, glass, etc.) and a sophisticated investor knows that a property's value can be improved with some tools and a little help. Property values can also be increased by changing its zoning or use, such as vacant lots being changed into parking lots, apartments into condos, or residential properties into a commercial zoning status. Each of these examples increases value and only requires creativity and effort.

Another awesome benefit to investing in real estate is the many tax benefits that are given by the government. The top three tax benefits of owning real estate worth mentioning are:

## 1. Deductible

- Tax laws allow various deductions for normal expenses incurred in the duration of owning real estate, such as:
- Upkeep.

- Maintenance.
- Improvements.
- Interest paid on the mortgage.

## 2. Depreciable

- Not only does tax law allow you to depreciate your investments, it requires it.
- It is presumed that things wear out and lose value over time.
- The government expects you to account for that wear and tear by claiming an annual decline in the value of the building, its contents, and any improvements, whether it is actually happening or not.
- This allows you to reduce your taxable income even when a property is increasing in value due to appreciation.

## 3. Deferrable

- Real estate permits the gain on any sale of an investment property to be transferred from the property you are selling to a new property being purchased.
- This defers the payment of any taxes on your transaction.
- The government has established these tax-deferring vehicles as a way for investors to reinvest real estate profits without having to pay those taxes until later.
- These programs help preserve your profits as you go, giving you more to reinvest.
- These programs help in accelerating the growth of your real estate portfolio.

Real estate is quite literally the only investment vehicle that puts a roof over your head. Your home can also be an investment, so you need to start seeing it for everything it can be. Your home is more than just your shelter; it is the foundation piece of your wealth-building path. There are many different paths available when it comes to building wealth via real estate. It is not uncommon for you to purchase and then move into a home, fix it up, and then rent it out when you're ready to move into a second home. While launching an investment career, you will be able to take care of a life necessity too. The bottom line here is that this can only happen with real estate.

Combine the benefits explored above and you will understand why real estate is the most powerful and best investment out there. Once I started investing in properties, I never stopped and I never will. I advise that you take advantage of real estate and its many benefits, and that you start investing as soon as possible. It's never too late to cash in on a good thing.

# *Chapter Highlights*

- Real estate is the safest, most reliable and most profitable investment.
- Residential properties are a much safer investment than commercial properties.
- Never put yourself in a position where you have to sell in a hurry!
- Choose one investing strategy and master it before moving on to another.
- Real estate provides the best ROI.
- Real estate is the key to building wealth.
- Even at 5% a year, appreciation can bring you wealth.
- It makes for a great retirement plan.
- Both your investment value and your rent prices will keep up with inflation increases.
- You can secure a second loan against the increased equity.
- You can refinance and pull out the equity in cash.
- It is deductible, depreciable, and deferrable.
- Start investing NOW.

*Chapter 5*

# THE WEALTHY BARMAID IS RESOURCEFUL IN SECURING TRADITIONAL & UNCONVENTIONAL FINANCING

W hen it comes to accruing enough money for down payments in a real estate purchase, there are so many options you can exercise. You should expect to put down at least 20% to 30% for residential properties. You should then expect to put down 25% to 50% of the purchase price for commercial properties. Please, be aware of all other options if you are putting down less than 20% on a real estate purchase. First, you will first need to understand how putting less money down can impact your cashflow. Secondly, you need to know how it can impede your ability to qualify for the next mortgage. Knowing all your options for down payments will optimize your investment strategy.

# Financing Options to Consider

1. Liquid assets
2. Equity from real estate
3. High-ratio insured mortgages
4. Subprime mortgages
5. Private money
6. Hard money
7. Seller financing/vendor take back (VTB)
8. Joint venture partnerships

# 1. Liquid Assets

This is the easiest and most desirable option. Liquid assets are any kind of money on hand that is readily available in cash form. It is also an investment that on short notice can easily be liquidated, like stocks or bonds, or anything that you think would be used more effectively as cash towards a real estate investment purchase. Having your own capital also makes you the most attractive to the banks, and keep in mind that by having your own capital you will be in the strongest position. You will not need to borrow or pay interest on an existing loan, nor will you need a partner to access any capital.

Because I worked consistently while saving 40% of my income for some time, I was able to purchase my first three properties with my own liquid assets. I achieved this without any kind of borrowing (for my down payments), just as my grandparents did for their first three houses. The more serious you become about investing, the more evident it becomes as to how quickly your money can get used up. If your plan is to purchase more than a couple properties a year (in the interest of keeping your portfolio growing) you will have to start looking at different options of raising capital.

# 2. Equity from Real Estate

If you own any real estate currently, a percentage of the money presently in your principal residence (or in other rental properties) can be used to fund part (if not all) of your down payment towards another property. A seasoned investor can calculate that accessible equity in your home with the following equation:

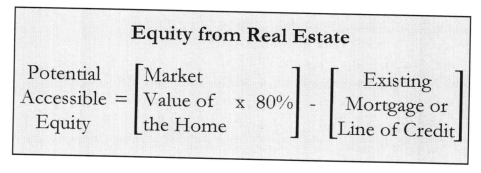

80% is the conventional lending limit before the mortgage is considered high-ratio and therefore requires insurance. Say the market value of your house is $200,000, and your outstanding mortgage (how much you still owe) is $100,000. 80% of the market value would be $160,000. You then subtract the $100,000 that you still owe on your mortgage from that, and you are left with $60,000 in equity which you can then withdraw. That is $60,000 in cash. This is refinancing, and I used this strategy numerous times on my rental properties in order to come up with down payments to purchase more real estate.

In my case, five years after purchasing one of my properties, I was able to pull out $53,000, and I was then able to put that $53,000 down towards another rental property. The market value of my house at that time was $230,000, and my existing mortgage was $108,000. The bank would finance me up to 70% because it was an investment property, not my principal residence.

---

**Equity from Real Estate:
Melanie's Example**

$$\text{Accessible Equity} = \left[\text{Market Value of Property} \times 70\%\right] - \left[\text{Outstanding Mortgage}\right]$$

$$= \left[\ \$230,000 \quad \times\ 70\%\right] - \left[\ \$108,000\ \right]$$

$$= \ \$53,000$$

---

I love how real estate constantly appreciates, and as investors I think this is one of the best benefits from investing in real estate. Appreciation gives you access to serious cash over time. Notice that I waited five years before withdrawing, and this is because my five-year fixed interest rate term was up for renewal. I did this ensuring that I would not be required to pay any kind of penalty for getting out of the five-year term.

If you know that you will need to pull money out within a shorter period of time, you also have the option of not locking yourself into a fixed term. If the rates are good enough, you can set a shorter term or keep the variable rate open. This will avoid any penalties when you need to gain access to the equity.

# 3. High-Ratio Insured Mortgages

This is where a company or broker finances your mortgage for more than 80% of the value. They sometimes finance up to 90%, or at least that used to be the case. They finance your mortgage with a pricey insurance policy, usually meaning that you will not need to come up with a down payment of 20%. High-ratio insured mortgages are very fluid and their policies change frequently depending on what is happening in the market.

In 2007, Canadian lenders and insurers were relaxing their lending rules to allow more American-style mortgage options. However, by 2008 the policy changed drastically and it was no longer an option to buy real estate with $0 down. Since then, it is also no longer an option to have a mortgage insured on a 40-year amortization by the Canadian Mortgage and Housing Commission (CMHC).

Even more change occurred in 2010 after the global recession; mortgages are now uninsurable for investment properties without 20% down. This rule change had no impact on commercial mortgages exclusively. This was not a bad thing necessarily, in my opinion. I am thankful that the Canadian banking system was never exposed to a great deal of subprime risk.

There was no major threat of a housing or mortgage meltdown in Canada, as was experienced by America. The US meltdown preceded a global crisis, one that led to banks all over the world tightening their lending, as well as their risk parameters. This enabled the Canadian banking system to revert back to its original, safe, and conservative system. Canada was rendered almost entirely unscathed during the subprime crisis.

The higher cost of a mortgage when it is financed at 95% really cuts into your cashflow. If you are having trouble getting your properties to cashflow with 20% down, imagine what happens with 5% down. Needless to say, it might be more of a challenge to come up with 20% for your purchases, but this is the right way to do it for your long-term success and wealth building goals. <u>The goal here is to make money, not lose it</u>. We can all agree on that, right?

When it comes to getting the deal or not, high-ratio insured mortgages still exist, and they are available to be used as part of your investment strategy if needed. They should only be considered <u>IF</u> you have exerted all other options. Please, remember to be very cautious when using them.

# 4. Subprime Mortgages

I know most of you have heard the term "subprime" many times in the last decade in a negative sense, but there is a distinction between what subprime means in Canada versus the colossal mess it was in the US. Since the crisis of 2008, many subprime options are now unavailable, but there are still some, and there will likely be more options offered in the years to come. Subprime simply means that the borrower, the candidate, or the lender of the mortgage is not prime. These lenders still operate today, and they offer some flexibility with stated income.

Their rules on verification of your income are more relaxed, benefiting those who are self-employed, or those with businesses who are still in the startup phases. Some lenders will be willing to offer up to 85%, but this can change monthly, so I recommend exercising different options first if at all possible. If you choose to use the subprime mortgage (usually to avoid putting 20% down), you will have to pay higher interest rates and fees. Because of this you might run into cashflow problems with your property (which is not ideal), but you will still be able to enjoy the many other benefits of being a real estate owner, including appreciation and of course the many tax benefits.

# 5. *Private Money*

When all other options of conventional lenders have been exhausted, your next option is to go to private lenders, and they will definitely be a more expensive alternative. If you are unable to qualify at a bank, private money is a legitimate alternative and it is worth considering, but it is expensive because interest rates for first mortgages will range from 7% to 10%, and second mortgages will range between 12% and 14%.

Much like subprime mortgages, there is more flexibility for self-employed individuals or business owners in their startup phase in terms of verifying their income. It allows loans based on the equity of the property, as much as on the strength of the borrower. However, this kind of money is not for everyone. Much like high-ratio insured mortgages, all other options should be exhausted before you consider a private lender.

If a less expensive conventional loan is not an option, private money can be invaluable for your business, as it allows you to keep your portfolio growing. If you know things will be changing with your financial situation soon, you can use private money for a short period of time, until perhaps you are suitable to qualify for a conventional mortgage with a traditional bank and switch over. If you use this strategy, you will receive the benefit of a much lower rate, which will greatly help your cashflow position.

# 6. *Hard Money*

Hard money loans are accompanied by high interest and fees, and they are a short-term, expensive option. These loans are typically issued by private investors or companies. The benefit of getting financing through a hard money lender is that the property value will be exclusively taken into account for qualification, and unlike private money, the credit worthiness of the borrower is not taken into account at all. This style of lending is purely asset-based, which is beneficial for those who do not have the best credit scores, are self-employed, or do not have high income.

Since the property itself is used as the only protection against default by the borrower, these loans have a lower loan-to-value (LTV) ratio than traditional loans. Hard money loans also carry interest rates even higher than a traditional subprime loan. Since traditional lenders do not make hard money loans, hard money lenders are sometimes private individuals who see value in these types of potentially risky ventures. These loans are typically used in turnaround situations, with very short-term financing. They are typically used by borrowers with poor credit but substantial equity in their property who wish to avoid foreclosure.

On the road to growing your portfolio, a benefit of using hard money is that the money is received so quickly that it allows you to make very quick purchasing decisions when needed. However, you should only use hard money if you have a fast exit strategy. These loans are used for projects that last from a few months to a few years, so unless you are planning on flipping a house or applying for a new loan from a conventional lender in the near future, I do not recommend using a hard money loan.

# 7. Vendor Take Back (VTB)

VTB is also known as seller financing. This is essentially a second mortgage that is arranged by the vendor/seller, in order to facilitate the purchase when the buyer does not have enough funds to close the deal. It is in your best interest to educate the vendor on the benefits that this option can bring to them.

For example, let's say that you do not have the 20% to put down on a real estate purchase. You approach the seller and ask them if they would hold a second mortgage on the property. The vendor can "take back" or grant you a portion of the down payment, usually around 10% in the form of a second mortgage.

If the purchase price is $150,000 and you have $15,000 (10%), you would arrange for a first mortgage with a conventional lender for $120,000. You would still be $15,000 short at this point. This is when you ask the vendor to grant you the remaining $15,000 in the form of a second mortgage charged against the property. You then negotiate the interest rate you will pay on the $15,000, and it will usually be a better rate than the vendor/seller would get by investing their money anywhere else; around a 7% to 10% return rate.

This situation works out nicely for the seller because their loan is secured against the property, making it a relatively safe investment. They will also have the ability to foreclose on you in the event that you default on your payments. Once they accept your offer, you then close the deal. You will simultaneously make payments to your bank for the first mortgage, as well as to your seller for the second. In this example, you will have now purchased your property with only 10% down.

You can also use seller financing for up to 100% of the purchase price. Doing this is more uncommon than a second mortgage with the seller. However, it is a viable strategy that can work well if your vendor does not owe anything on their mortgage. Seller financing works especially well when they own the property free and clear. With a vendor take back, you will both execute a promissory note providing a rate of interest, a schedule of repayment, and any consequences of defaulting. You simply need to educate the seller/vendor on the benefits this can provide them, and you need to pay them an attractive interest rate.

There is a certain appeal to cutting out the middle man (banks and mortgage lenders) and having the seller finance the entire transaction instead. Where else can a seller receive 5% to 10% rate of return with almost no risk? Their investment is backed by a tangible asset. These arrangements are usually short-term ones, since most sellers will not want the hassle of collecting payments from anyone for the next thirty years.

A typical deal might be for the loan to be amortized for thirty years with a balloon payment after five years. A balloon payment refers to the repayment of the outstanding principal sum, made at the end of the loan period. Once you successfully make your payments for those five years, conventional lenders will be more likely to consider you for a more traditional loan. In terms of timeline, if you choose VTB or seller financing, I recommend that you exercise the same strategy that I suggested with a private lender.

Some benefits of VTB include the fact that a seller might give you a "mortgage" even if a more traditional lender has turned you down. The closing process is faster and cheaper, and the down payment can be whatever amount the both of you agree upon. I have seen some cases with $0 down, which is rare, but it is still very much a possibility in today's market. If you pursue this option to finance your purchase, ensure that you use a real estate lawyer (in addition to a real estate agent), who can write a sales contract and promissory note effectively. This will cover you for any liability.

# 8. Joint Venture Partnerships

This method is one of the most popular in real estate investing. It establishes the investor as the expert, and they will do all the work, finding the property, closing the deal, as well as finding another party willing to invest funds into the property for a healthy return. The investor will also handle negotiations and management of the property, whether you are keeping it (for a buy and hold) or flipping it later. Usually, the other party brings funding for the down payment and the closing costs. Both parties usually go on title and are responsible for the mortgage.

A Joint Venture (JV) Agreement can be for any percentage you negotiate together. Your typical JV Agreement splits both the monthly cashflow and the net proceeds from any future sale 50/50. This agreement will be the best solution for investors who have limited capital but still want to acquire multiple properties for their investment portfolio. There are unlimited opportunities for growth with this method if it is used properly. Joint Venture Agreements are one of the fastest and highest leveraged investment tools available.

## Key Points to Attracting a Joint Venture Partner

It starts with building your Joint Venture Proposal (your business plan), which is a very important tool for raising money from potential investors. You need to show your proposal to a potential venture partner, and explain to them how this deal will make them money, and when the deal will return their capital.

In order to find these people, you need to build a list of potential investors. These investors might be in your current network already, some of whom you may never have approached before, but they are currently in your community. You will ideally reach out to them and ask permission to contact them when you have a deal under contract. Once the legwork is done and you have a deal all tied up, you will then bring it to them, shopping your deal to every potential investor on that list.

Once you have at least one investor interested and committed, this is when you sign a JV Agreement. You will then personally carry on through the process of arranging financing, closing the deal, and managing the property. After the deal is closed, you will be able to carry out your intentions.

It is important not to be greedy when dealing with partnerships of any kind, and I think it is important that we always strive to give more than we receive. Your potential investors will now have trusted you through a deal, and at that point you should reward your partners for investing in you. This is a fantastic long-term strategy that you should practice, because in the long run, you will eventually have investors on your list who are always ready, willing, and happy to fund more deals with you in the future. These investors will know that when you come knocking, they always make money.

# Creativity Wins the Day

There are many ways of getting involved with real estate investing whether you have money or not. Again, the only thing stopping you from getting into the game is your own fear, limitations, and mindset. Another obstacle slowing you down might be a lack of imagination. Anyone, regardless of their financial situation or skill level, can at least begin the road to building wealth with real estate. Now is the time to get innovative with the various financial strategies that are available to help you reach your goals. To begin, you just need some financial education, as well as an open and creative mind.

# *Chapter Highlights*

- Expect to put down 20-30% for a down payment on residential property.
- Expect to put down 25-50% on commercial properties.
- Liquid assets are the strongest option for financing your investments.
- With the equity you have built up in your property, you can refinance your mortgage and withdraw 70-80% of the equity – in cash.
- While subprime mortgages come with higher interest rates and fees, you will be able to enjoy the benefits of being a real estate property owner.
- If you know things will be changing with your financial situation soon, you can use a private/hard money loan for a short period of time, until perhaps you are suitable to qualify for a conventional mortgage with a traditional bank.
- You should only use hard money if you have a fast exit strategy.
- Some benefits of VTB include:
- The fact that a seller might give you a "mortgage" even if a more traditional lender has turned you down.
- The closing process is faster and cheaper.
- The down payment can be whatever amount the both of you agree upon.
- Do not be greedy when it comes to JV partners, and ensure that you consistently reward them.
- You must get creative with available strategies to finance your investments.
- There are options for everyone.

*Chapter 6*

# THE WEALTHY BARMAID HABITUALLY GROWS HER NETWORK

Who you surround yourself with is who you will become. If you hang around five millionaires, you will be the sixth. If you hang around five broke people, you will also be the sixth. Reed Hoffman (co-founder of LinkedIn) once said, "The fastest way to change yourself is to hang out with people who are already the way you want to be." Networking is a powerful tactic to accelerate and sustain success for any of us. Many high-powered and wealthy people admit that they owe every job, and every opportunity along the way, to networking.

For many people, networking has delivered more ROI than any other business tool. Remember, there is no instant gratification with networking; it is something that takes time. Yes, there have been those one chance meetings where everything clicks and everyone walks away with a brilliant but random contact. This scenario can occur, but it is not the norm. Networking is truly focused on human relationships, and these do not necessarily develop quickly. Relationships take time and effort. Connecting with people is a balance of sharing, where the support and information that you receive should be equal to what you are giving.

When networking, you must remain persistent: <u>Do not give up</u>. Before any venue seems either beneficial or fruitless, you need to keep circulating, because you need to have access to places that attract likeminded individuals, and you need to consistently attend those options for exposure. As I previously covered in my sixth habit (surrounding yourself with as many likeminded/motivated people as possible), I advise that you make it a personal habit to attend as many events as possible, and activate it as part of your weekly, monthly, or yearly routine.

Once you build this habit, and you are regularly implementing it, <u>keep going</u>. Once again, this is about getting yourself repeat exposure, and then building stronger relationships with whomever you connect. The overall goal here is building and maintaining long term relationships with likeminded people, as well as putting yourself in environments surrounded by those that inspire you. Your network is the people who will help you grow by interaction. You will learn from them, and you will pick up new and current ideas, concepts, strategies, and solutions.

The more you interact, the more people you will meet through those connections for potential business collaborations. Being around these growth-focused mindsets will get you excited for creating awesome things, which is a very positive benefit from putting yourself out there. This exposure will motivate you to improve within any area you are already working in. Remember, you need to add value to everyone you meet and connect with, and focus on what you are giving more than what you are receiving. In the big picture, this mindset will take you a lot further in both life and in business.

My grandfather was a pro at networking. He practically knew everyone in any city that he ever lived or had business in, and everyone knew him too. He has been a great model to watch, because he always builds meaningful relationships with people. He is a man who both genuinely cares about people, and loves developing profound connections with them, which he still does to this day. He always takes the time to help anyone who needs it, and he definitely always gives more than he receives. He taught me that this is how you succeed in life.

My grandfather never missed an opportunity to get out there and meet new people. He would talk to people, get to know them, and develop relationships anywhere that he could, and his success was in great part due to this. Over time he built a network around himself with individuals from vastly different backgrounds and industries. He is now always prepared for anything new, because he has the right connections, or the right people to guide him in whatever endeavor he pursues. He will never stop creating and nurturing those relationships.

My uncle is another great example of a networking master. On a weekly basis, he consistently attends charity events, social functions, and business affairs. Since I was young, he always invited me to award ceremonies, gala events, and community rallies. Through him, I was able to grow and expand my own network in the area. I met all kinds of local leaders, bankers, brokers, lawyers, and other corporate professionals. I would never know who I would meet when I went with him, and he would always remind me that I never knew who I might end up needing in the future. At the time, I was eighteen and I did not need anyone's help, but at twenty-seven I then had the contacts that I needed to enter a new phase on my journey towards financial freedom.

Networking is not about talking to people when you need something. It is about talking to people in preparation for the day when you may need something, be it advice, influence, capital, or any combination thereof. Since I was a teenager, I have valued seeking out, creating, building, and developing relationships. From the days of attending events with my uncle, I knew two things:

1.  I wanted to be an entrepreneur and create something great in my life.
2.  An extensive network of successful, likeminded/motivated individuals was one of the most important assets that I could ever have.

As I have grown up since then, I have attended a variety of events, and I have connected with people from all over the world in a variety of industries. Each of these gatherings taught me how to interact with many different people of diverse backgrounds, both socially and professionally. Sure, I was a little nervous starting off, but in putting myself out there and talking to people, I realized that each person attending is a human being, and we were all there in an attempt to create relationships and familiarize ourselves with one another.

Over the years, I developed friendships with doctors, lawyers, financiers, and big business entrepreneurs. I have been a student of life, taking in everything that I heard from those professionals and entrepreneurs. I could not get enough of being around likeminded people, and I learned so much from each of them, such as:

1. What their best business habits were.
2. When and how they were investing their money. This almost always includes real estate.
3. How different market economies affected their respective businesses.
4. The intricacies of various businesses operations.

I harnessed many connections and relationships over the course of my young adulthood. Each of them taught me new ways of interacting with people from other industries. The more I was around these connections, the more often I learned new things, stretching and inspiring my mind.

Using the same principles, as I learned from networking with my uncle, I also interacted with my professors while I was in university. My relationships with them opened up many opportunities for me beyond graduation. A few of them later asked me to speak in front of their marketing and entrepreneurship classes. Presenting to my professors' students was my first experience with public speaking. I absolutely loved everything about those visits, and through them I made even more connections.

Also, since I was a teenager, I volunteered for many charities, even sitting on a few boards, where I made deep connections with the other people involved. Each of my relationships there easily formed because everyone there was working towards the same cause, donating their time, energy, and efforts together. In my experience with charities, the relationships formed there have been lasting and very meaningful. I made many friends along the way, and there were many opportunities born from those relationships.

Over time, through networking with so many people from such a variety of industries, I found:

1. Job opportunities both in Toronto as well as in my hometown
2. Many real estate leads
3. Business leads
4. Banking and financing connections
5. Public speaking opportunities
6. Advice and guidance
7. Support and motivation
8. Increased business for my gastro pub

While I did create meaningful friendships from meetings with people at events and functions, it was not always this way. It took some time to figure it out on my own, and there was certainly a time when I stayed within the limits of my fears and comfort zone. I have been guilty of keeping certain friends or acquaintances for too long. I did not realize there were certain people in my life who were hindering my happiness and my success, who were shortsighted, narrow-minded, and negative.

After a while I realized that they were not helping me grow or progress in any area of my life. On the contrary, they were holding me back. I knew then that I needed to change course if I wanted to reach my desired outcome. I started immediately attending events, meet-ups, seminars, classes, and workshops. I would even attend intensive multiple-day live conferences, boot camps, intensive training sessions, mastermind groups, trade shows, and so on.

Keep in mind, I did not limit myself to my local area. I also went to many cities across the United States. As I attended these functions, I found and connected with more likeminded individuals, entrepreneurs, as well as young professionals. I will not say that every event or relationship was quality or long-lasting, but I knew that it would just take time.

# *Four Benefits of Networking*

The more you do anything in life and the more time, energy, and effort that you put into harnessing relationships, the more you will see over time that everything compounds. Over the course of networking, you will build connections with great people whom you will then surround yourself with, and maintain contact with.

I found people who had their own aspirations, dreams, positivity, and an enthusiasm for life. I met go-getters who did their work extremely well, who would never settle for a life of mediocrity. I met people who challenged and stimulated me intellectually, and professionals who were not all talk; each of them did whatever it was that they set out to do. From the start, I wanted to align myself with these types of people, because I knew there was nothing better than having a network of likeminded/ motivated colleagues around you who have a serious enthusiasm for life, who get out there day after day chasing their dreams.

There is nothing more encouraging than having a network of people who are actively growing themselves. Each of you will work hard to make your respective dreams a reality. The people you choose to spend time with have a profound effect on your work as well as your life, and you need to take that very seriously by always choosing the people in your life wisely. This is about forming relationships on trust, because you are helping one another towards your goals. Regularly engaging with your contacts, and finding opportunities to assist them will strengthen your relationships. By doing this, you are sowing the seeds for reciprocal assistance when you need help in achieving goals of your own.

There are many benefits from networking that will not only help you succeed professionally, but will also improve your quality of life. The four major benefits covered in this section are as follows:

1.  Leads and increased business
2.  Advice and support
3.  Raising your reputation
4.  Friendship

## *Leads & Increased Business*

Your ROI with networking can take the form of <u>opportunities</u>. Does that word sound like gold to you yet? In my opinion, opportunities are priceless. If you think that you are not getting enough opportunities, then now is the time to start nurturing your relationships, and networking regularly.

A network can bring you:

- Joint ventures
- Client leads
- Partnerships
- Speaking engagements
- Employment opportunities
- Businesses
- Assets

The great part about network-generated leads is that the referrals you receive will be high quality, and most of the time they are prequalified. When you follow up on those referrals or leads, you will then be able to turn them into clients. Your network will provide much higher quality leads than any other form of marketing.

Remember that you need to reciprocate with the contacts you make. You will connect people with each other, and help others grow their businesses too. Personally, I experienced this benefit many times, not only with my gastro pub, but also in real estate. Many deals came to me from my network through the contacts I have made that I never would have known or heard about, or benefited from otherwise.

## *Advice & Support*

We rely on our networks (when we are not using Google) for advice and guidance, and this keeps us on track. Keep in mind that as you receive advice, you also need to give advice back to your network in return. The better you become at networking, the more knowledge you can tap into. These relationships can help you avoid making unfortunate or costly mistakes, and they can put you on the right path. When you are confused or need a little direction, this alone can save you years and tons of money by shortening the learning curve.

Networking provides an opportunity to exchange best practice knowledge, where you can learn about the business techniques of your peers. Through each of your connections, you will stay abreast of the latest industry developments. A wide network of informed, interconnected contacts means broader access to new and valuable information.

Supportive people around you are an invaluable resource, especially when you are an entrepreneur. Your role as the decision maker, bread winner, and overall renegade usually happens as a party of one, and that being said, the entrepreneurial road can be very lonely. When things are going well, many along this road are unaware of the absence of support and perspective. The truth is that any entrepreneur needs the perspective of other entrepreneurs, friends, mentors, and coaches. We need people around us who get it and are wired the same way.

It is critical to have peers and collaborators to interact with and discuss important issues along your path. Discussing common challenges and opportunities opens the door to valuable suggestions and guidance. Offering genuine assistance to your contacts also sets a strong foundation for receiving support in return when you are in need of it.

## *Raising Your Reputation*

Being visible and getting noticed is essential for professional development, and this is a benefit of networking that puts you on the map in business. The more connections that you make and the more you expose yourself to many different settings, the closer you will be to both finding and attracting the right people with whom to associate. The more associated you become, the closer you will be to people who can help you along your path to success.

Networking is not just about going one time; it requires more of you. Regularly attending business and social events is vital in getting your face known, your talent recognized, and your work and contribution noticed. If you are attending these events regularly, it helps build your professional reputation as knowledgeable, reliable, and supportive. As people are giving advice and information to you, in turn you should also give useful information and tips to people who need it as well. Once again, you need to ensure that you are not just benefiting from your connections; they need to benefit from you as well.

By consistently being around these circles you are more likely to receive leads, referrals, partners, or business opportunities. Consistent attendance often leads to you popping into a person's head when they need what you have to offer. They might also connect you with someone who complements what you do.

## *Friendship*

We should never forget the important benefit of friendship that can result from networking. This area does not convert into dollars, pounds or euros, but do not overlook the benefit of having friends with a similar interest. There is so much benefit to being surrounded by like minds with no strings attached. Life can be and will be difficult. In those rough patches, it is imperative to have people who are there for us in any event. Friends can keep you motivated and positive; especially ones who understand you on a psychological and emotional level. Friendship is worth more than gold, especially when you are on a similar path.

# Four Venues for Quality Networking

Now that the benefits of networking have been covered, it is time to explore the best places to get started. I have enjoyed many different kinds of events, at all kinds of venues where I met a variety of friends, colleagues, mentors, and coaches. There are also a plethora of events that you can find online through websites and URL communities.

There are services like Event Bright, and Meet-Up, which have a selection of groups, both professional as well as social. From the comfort of your home, you can browse through lists of opportunities, where there are many to be found. Pick any of the groups that interest you, and then check them out in person.

The goal with these services is to explore new circles of people, and new venues that you might enjoy. You then nurture those connections by consistently attending events with each other, because sharing a common interest will help make bonding with each other much easier. If you regularly attend events with groups like these, you will be able to create deeper connections in the relationships that you discover therein.

To get you started, here are some venues to pay attention to:

1. Industry events
2. Chamber of commerce
3. Classes and seminars
4. Leisure activities

# *Industry Events*

These include trade shows, conventions, and conferences where you will find likeminded people, because everyone attending also works in your field – and each of them share common interests and knowledge. Industry events are excellent places for meeting potential collaborators, friends, business partners, investors, and mentors.

The energy in the air around these events gets your creative juices flowing, because it is exciting to be around so many people working towards something great. Being in this type of atmosphere gives you momentum and drive, providing the motivation needed to get you through whatever stage you are dealing with, and into the next level of your path. Every idea and concept, all the knowledge available, and the people themselves can open your mind to both higher levels of thinking as well as higher levels of achievement.

# *Chamber of Commerce*

Another area worth spending time in includes your local chamber of commerce or similar associations. These groups make a point of hosting local meetings, seminars, events, and presentations. Likeminded people from your area will be in attendance, so you will be in an environment with compatible individuals who are also interested in developing and growing their businesses.

These potential connections will also have an interest in the immediate economy around them. Being around these kinds of people will be beneficial to your growth and success as an entrepreneur. And it will benefit you to be an active member of your local community.

## Classes and Seminars

When you are learning something new along with everyone else, breaking the ice is a non-issue. You can help each other in understanding a concept, perhaps by borrowing books or materials. You might even arrange some kind of accountability or mastermind group.

The class teacher or speaker is also a great person to network with. They will have information, insight, knowledge, and connections that can greatly benefit you. You can take a class on just about any topic, in any given city. You have no excuses for not learning something new and connecting with other people.

## Leisure Activities

Leisure is not often associated with your professional or investing career, but you will be surprised where your ideas and contacts may originate from. Some of the best breakthroughs emerge from pretty unusual places. Again, networking is much easier when there is a common interest, so leisure activities where you might find that include:

- Hobby groups
- Retreats
- Sports leagues
- Team activities
- Art groups
- Book clubs
- Volunteer work (Kiwanis International and Rotary International, for instance)

Networking during a leisure activity works especially well, as neither you nor anyone else taking part are consciously thinking about work. The basis of a shared leisure activity allows everyone to naturally get acquainted as people, before getting to know each other professionally, creating more opportunity for the formation of more personal bond and connection in a leisure-focused setting. Again, you need to put yourself out there as much as possible.

# The Wealthy Barmaid's Ideal Network Includes

Networking is the same in all fundamental aspects, but you need to get the concept a little more tailored to your vision for your real estate investing business. Your current network may already be helpful in this regard. All successful investors have relationships with people who send them support, opportunities, and mentors. They have relationships with people who help them purchase and maintain their properties. In many cases, these connections provide services that will enable investors to do more while spending less time and effort.

As a business person, I call this exchange "leverage." With qualified help, you will accomplish more than you ever could accomplish alone. Even if you are only purchasing a few properties, you need to start establishing a dream team for your investment career. This team should include:

1.  Close professionals
2.  Fiduciary professionals
3.  Independent contractors and freelancers

You will need help from real estate agents, contractors, brokers, lenders, accountants, lawyers, and property managers (yes, all of them). You need these team members to ensure that you are doing things safely, reliably, and profitably. Sophisticated real estate investors will not succeed without the help of others. For every successful investor you know, there is a team of people working behind the scenes. Your dream network should be an intentionally recruited group of people who will each play a specific role in helping you, the investor, succeed.

An investor's network is critical for success. These groups of interconnected people, who each play a specific and active role in real estate investments, should be an expert at what they do. Each of them will give you information, advice, guidance, wisdom, instruction, mentoring, strategy, contacts, connections, leads, leverage, and labor. Each member of your team should be willing to help when needed.

This is about forming a personal and strategic wealth-building team. This section is where you go about finding all the people you need for each part of the process. Here, you will learn everything you need to know, and finish everything you need to get done.

Your real estate investing network is very important to your future wealth-building goals. The members of this group will help you from beginning to end with your transactions, so before you get to investing, set your team up first; this way you will be on the front end of good decisions, instead of on the back end of desperate ones. You will be more likely to make great decisions quickly, because you will not have to slow down and go looking for the right people. Remember, if you want to be the best investor that you can possibly be, you need to surround yourself with the best network.

# Close Professionals

You need to actively, purposefully, and selectively build powerful working relationships with professionals who are closest to you currently, who are long term and mutually beneficial. This network is ideally composed of professionals who are already committed to you – the ones who care about your financial success and your wellbeing. They should each have more knowledge, experience, and success with investing and finances than you do, because you will need each of them to mentor and guide you.

Think of this group as your informal board of directors for building wealth, and for real estate investment decisions. They will not only help you professionally, but also personally. If there is something that you are unsure of, they will tell you what you need to know, or they will connect you with someone who does. If you need a partner, they will become that person or they will find someone who will. In any investment endeavor, they will broaden their way of helping you, or they will find you someone who can.

# Fiduciary Professionals

As a real estate investor, these people look out for your best interests in all your transactions and dealings. They have the ability to manage each transaction piece for you, and if need be, they can manage all of them. This network forms the foundation of the professional team on whom you will rely, and they will be with you through every transaction.

These professionals are the real estate agents, lenders, accountants, and lawyers who will be brought in on every opportunity in an important way. These are key individuals in all transactions handled by you. You need to ensure these team members are the best at what they do, because these are areas that can really harm you and your success via legalities, lawsuits, and CRA/IRS issues. To avoid any problems, ensure that these experts are at the top of their field when choosing them for your dream team.

## Independent Contractors and Freelancers

These are members of your team who perform specific functions for your particular properties or transactions. They are the inspectors, appraisers, insurance agents, electricians, painters, roofers, plumbers, landscapers, and any professional you might need depending on the situation. They are the skilled experts who will provide specific services needed in order to close and maintain your investments. Remember, what they do, how well they do it, and what they charge for doing it can make or break your deal.

As always, you need to be very intentional and precise as to whom you bring onto your team. Make sure that you do your proper due diligence and research each and every one of them. Use your advisors for advice and guidance on finding and choosing these professionals.

# The Wealthy Barmaid's Dream Team

You might wonder how and where you will find these people. There are venues that are specific to networking in real estate such as conferences, associations, clubs, groups, investment networks, and those that are real estate specific. Likewise, there are many real estate communities, mentoring programs, coaches, and websites that you can check out and get involved with. Most towns have these networks and associations, so there are many opportunities all around you for meeting and developing relationships. There are also a multitude of opportunities for learning and gaining useful information along the way.

These places usually give a lot of relevant information to all things real estate. Each of the venues explored are great for surrounding yourself with people who are on a similar journey as you, and in the same industry no less. The people you meet will be more than happy to talk with you, and share information with you. There are many who will be open to further building a relationship or even collaborating on a potential project with you.

Your network will be a great group of people to ask for recommendations and suggestions on particular professionals you might want to approach for joining your team on your path to building wealth through real estate. My dream team was built through trial and error because I was quite young when I started investing. My mistakes were pretty costly, and I wish I had known of these things back then.

If I knew then what I do now, I would have saved a lot of money and I could have avoided the headache of it all, but I learned from my mistakes. I became wiser about meeting and working with the right people. Networking in this particular setting enabled me to ask fellow investors:

- Who is the best person in your field?
- Who has a great track record?
- Who do you advise I work with?

I made it my mission to find the top players so I could recruit them to my team. I was successful in finding fantastic people to work with, and I am in a very comfortable place now. I have a team that I love; one that gets the job done right. Having experts on your team is priceless in my opinion, and I worked hard to attract the ones I have on mine. I also took the time and effort to grow and nurture each of those relationships, and I became very close with the people on my team. I speak to my lawyer, my real estate agent, my lenders, and my accountants on a weekly and sometimes even daily basis. We communicate frequently, sometimes in matters completely unrelated to real estate.

My team has become more than just a circle of professional colleagues and associates. We have become close friends. I nurture those relationships frequently not only because I respect them for their amazing work, but also because I value the relationships that we have created and developed over time. Together, we have weathered storms, fought battles, and closed many important deals.

# *The Wealthy Barmaid's Rules of Engagement*

Once I develop a network, I will harness and maintain those relationships for the rest of my investing and business life. So too will you need to stay as active in maintaining and nurturing your own network. To help you stay active in this, these are my rules of engagement:

1. Always keep your word
2. Never speak negatively about anyone
3. Never short change anyone you work with
4. Keep doing deals
5. Refer business to your network members
6. Always give more than you receive

Networking is about building solid relationships, and a reputation that people can trust.

> [Relationships] + [Reputation] = Deals.

As you may already know, relationships are built on communication, cooperation, collaboration, and your track record. In order to maintain those relationships, give each member of your dream team a monthly phone call at the very least. In this call, find out how they are doing, and share what you've been up to. When you are all caught up, talk about real estate investing.

For the closest members of your team, make an effort of meeting up with them in person, again, at least once a month. You can schedule a quick visit to their office or take them to coffee or lunch. Your goal is to tell them what you are doing, and then ask for any advice or guidance that you might need. You should also ensure that you offer any assistance they might need from you. You will keep each other abreast of any deals or opportunities that might be in the trenches.

Reputation is one of the most important factors in real estate investing. This will take a little longer to build until you develop a proven track record for yourself. With that in mind, you must prove your record by following the six rules of engagement listed above, because they will help you develop and maintain a great reputation. If you have a good track record, people will want to do business with you, and they will be happy to help you in your times of need.

# *Chapter Highlights*

- Your net worth is the sum total of the five people you hang around with the most.
- Networking delivers more return on investment than any other tool in business.
- Explore the options around you:
- Venues
- Events
- Groups
- Make networking a habit and <u>be consistent</u>.
- Get out there.
- Go to events, conferences, and meet ups.
- Build and maintain long-term relationships with people you connect with.
- Always focus on giving more than you receive.
- Build a team specific to your real estate investing goals (your dream team).
- Protect your reputation.

*Chapter 7*

# THE WEALTHY BARMAID DEEPLY VALUES THE IMPORTANCE OF HER MENTORS

One of the key ingredients to success in any career is finding and building relationships with mentors. You need to find the professionals who are stretching, searching, and seeking a higher ground in life; who will also open your mind to new possibilities. You need to find those who are beyond your current realm of thinking, because they will guide you along your wealth-building path safely, reliably, and of course, profitably.

The influence that a mentor can have on your life is priceless. Your mentor will have achieved the level of success that you admire and aspire towards, and because you will then have access to their wisdom, they can help you in so many ways. They will help you further yourself to new heights in your career path, and you will reach levels that would not have previously occurred to you. Mentors and coaches are also great resources for contacts and connections who can help you along your path. This undoubtedly increases your visibility, credibility, and results. As I covered in the previous chapter, this opens doors and enriches your industry network for more opportunities.

There are different kinds of mentors and coaches, from personal, professional, to educational. You might pick mentors from the people who are already a part of your life, who you are already close with, and who you already see on a regular basis. There are mentors you can find through structured coaching companies or programs, where you pay for mentoring/coaching services, and each of them have a ton of value and are worth exploring, depending on your specific needs.

Again, you may already have a few people in your life that can help you find solutions for any barriers that you are currently facing. People like these can provide you with any information you might need. There are people out there who can give guidance as you are moving forward with your goals and aspirations, and my advice is that you begin your search with your friends, family, colleagues, acquaintances, coworkers, and generally people who you trust. From time to time, you should ask them for advice, just to make sure you are on the right track and to avoid making any huge mistakes along the way.

Before you begin your search, let's outline a few specifics so you can find the right mentors for you:

1. What level of assistance do you need?
2. Who do you respect?
3. Who can challenge you?
4. Who will hold you accountable?
5. Who can help you progress?

## *What Level of Assistance Do You Need?*

What is your desired depth of learning? If you discover that you need more devoted attention in reaching your goals, you should consider paying for coaching or mentoring services in whichever realm you are specifically trying to get into. This route is usually more in depth, with more hand-holding along the way. Coaches and mentors will spend a lot of time with you, and they will help you map out and form strategic plans to achieve success.

Mentors will provide an abundance of benefits by working side by side with you until you reach your achievement, holding you accountable and pushing you to your limits. It all depends on the level of attention you require or have in mind. It depends on whatever stage of the game you are currently in, and what your needs are. You need to assess your environment in order to know which set of mentors you might need.

When engaging professional coaching services, you will be more likely to hold yourself accountable and stay focused because you will be spending both your time and your money. In comparison to a college course, your mentor will not give you a grade, any quizzes, or a midterm. Your mentor will give you something more valuable: advice, feedback, and strategies. There are no tests because you are already working on your own business, and their intention is to get you from point A to B through guidance, support, and accountability. Your results will not need grading, because the only viable comparison that will take place is:

What was your desired outcome?

VS.

What did you accomplish?

## *Who Do You Respect?*

One sound piece of advice from a mentor can be the catalyst that changes your frame of reference forever. One "aha" moment can propel you forward faster than a year of steady work. While your friends and peers can share their intuition and their perceptions with you (yes, there are benefits from this), you need to be careful about who you take advice from.

You need someone with a proven track record of success. When it comes to mentors, if you respect their experience, success and wisdom, you are more likely to accept and value their insights. You will actually apply these with a greater sense of urgency, which brings you results faster and more efficiently.

## *Who Can Challenge You?*

As you work with a mentor, you will find yourself being pushed and challenged. Often a seasoned mentor can challenge you to think in ways that never occurred to you. They might also give you a necessary push in taking a leap. Mentors will pull you out of your comfort zone and encourage you to think unconventionally. They have seen more of the world, and they have more business experience than you. A mentor has been innovating as well as solving problems for a much longer time than you. While they may not always have the answer, if you allow them to bolster your experience with their own, you will inherit some cleverness from the manner in which they operate.

After working with a mentor, you will be more confident in your actions than if you continued alone. As you achieve your goals, you will earn their respect too. As you begin to see yourself as a peer to your coach or mentor, you will be amazed at how your self-esteem and confidence will grow as a result.

## Who Will Hold You Accountable?

Motivation can be a hard thing to manufacture. In announcing that you will achieve something to your mentor, you have now set yourself a goal. In sharing your goal with your mentor, you now have someone who will hold you accountable. This means you are more likely to create action and therefore see results quickly. If you have a good mentor or coach, they will push your limits, and they will stretch your thinking as well as your comfort levels. It will inspire and motivate you along your journey because you will have someone in your corner.

## Who Can Help You Progress?

Mentors can help you do more with your strengths, to capitalize on your hidden talents in ways that you may never have seen before. Again, when you are struggling, asking friends and coworkers for advice can be helpful, but a mentor will be more likely to give you entirely different perspectives from anyone who knows you personally. They offer you impartial advice from a strategic point of view, and that kind of interaction can help you see the opportunities and challenges from a more constructive perspective.

Mentors will help you develop solutions much faster. When you gain valuable business advice, you shorten your learning curve, and this is integral for saving time and money. When you have a problem at work, a mentor can advise you, and they will work with you to navigate the problem in a professional way. Their experience and insight will also stop you from making any major mistakes, as they will give you the answer as opposed to you making a crucial mistake and wasting valuable time, energy, effort, frustration, and money learning from it. They will help you construct a better way to handle the situation, and avoid disasters.

# *Mentors of the Wealthy Barmaid*

If you want to have an acknowledged mentoring relationship (specifically from the people who are already in your life) all you need to do is ask. Go to people you respect, tell them that you admire their judgment and business skills, and that you would like to learn from them. Ask if you can impose on their time for answers to some questions you might have. When I ask this way, nobody turns me down. You'll find that a vast majority of experienced business people you approach will say yes. Mentoring is actually fun for them, because they get to pass on their expertise. They often enjoy the process.

Any time that I need more in-depth (paid) mentoring and coaching, I start by researching the specific realm of coaching that I need. Once I identify the specifics, I will start asking around my network to see if there is any feedback for any organizations or people in particular that they have worked with before (covering any topic, strategic business, real estate investment, marketing and branding, or wealth building). When I have some names, I reach out to them. After some communication, I will choose the best fit, and then I get started right away. I make this decision quickly because the speed of implementation will determine how successful (or not) I will become.

As I mentioned before, my uncle was one of my earliest mentors, along with one of my cousins. When I was twenty-three, I had my first experience with a business coach for about $200 an hour. For me, that was a lot of money at the time, but I saw the value in fast-tracking my learning from someone who was already where I wanted to be.

I have worked with many mentors and coaches specific to business strategy and development. I always invest in myself, my education, self-improvement, and self-development, because I believe these things are extremely valuable. Education is an investment in yourself, and I have highly valued each and every tidbit of information that I have gained along the way. Adding mentors to my life who have achieved the levels of success I want to achieve always has a profound impact on my success and my progress.

Working with mentors allowed me to shave years off of my personal journey, and I saved a lot of money from their shared knowledge and wisdom. I was able to skip the mistakes they themselves have made in the past. Mentors give me efficient ways of doing what I need to do in order to get to where I need to go quickly.

Each of my mentors brings such a wide range of experience to the table, and having access to this provides such a fantastic guide to help me stay on course. Some of my mentors have catapulted me into a higher level of success much faster than I would ever have experienced alone. My route is to find someone who has already achieved what I want, and then I pay them for an accelerated education. I find that paying someone for help and guidance is much cheaper in the long run.

Your other option is the old trial-and-error method, which can be very frustrating as well as expensive. You will run the risk of getting lost in the chaos while making all kinds of mistakes as you try to figure it all out alone. Believe me, I once approached things with a trial-and-error mindset, and I regretted it afterward.

# The Wealthy Barmaid's Uncle

Aside from paid mentors and coaches, my uncle has been a business mentor of mine since as far back as I can remember. He taught me so much about business, real estate, and building wealth. As I mentioned in Chapter Six, he also taught me the importance of networking and building relationships with a variety of people in multiple industries.

My uncle also taught me how to negotiate deals and seek opportunities. As with most of my family, he believes real estate is the best path for building wealth. Early in my life, I recognized the value of spending as much time with my uncle as possible, and observing all things business. His office was my second home as I sat in on so many of his business meetings since I was a teenager. I would work with him on some of his bigger projects out of pure curiosity regarding business in general. There is nothing like a hands-on learning atmosphere.

My uncle is one of those anomalies in life that I will always admire. He spots diamonds in the rough, and literally makes something from nothing. He will search for properties and businesses that no one else has an interest in, or that everyone else is fearful of, and then he will turn them into something that people will pay premium prices to buy. People generally avoid the properties or businesses he goes after because they had previously failed or no one could make them work.

My uncle is one of the most determined businessmen I have ever had privilege of knowing. He will never say "no" to hearing about an opportunity or listening to what someone has to say. He believes in taking the time to entertain or listen to anyone who wants to bring something to the table. "You never know where that relationship might lead to in the future" he says. Even if the current deal is not one he is interested in, he will never say, "I don't have the time" or "I'm too busy." He always takes the time, even though he has more active deals, properties, businesses, and companies than the majority of people I know put together!

I learned so much from him and I still do to this day. I never take it for granted that I have such a smart and successful role model to learn from, and I am a sponge whenever it comes to his words of wisdom. I listen carefully and I watch intently; I value each and every piece of advice he gives me, and most importantly, I apply the lessons I am taught. I used to pester him so much, going into his office to talk about opportunities or ask for advice every day. Sometimes I would simply go and sit in on his meetings because I enjoyed seeing how he negotiated and closed deals. I would learn so much from watching how he dealt with all sorts of people and different opportunities; in fact, I still sit in on his meetings.

I learned about mortgages, financing, partnerships, and how to operate businesses, all from a very young age, thanks to him. He is the biggest reason that I became an entrepreneur, and why I invest in real estate today. If I had never shown an interest in learning about business or real estate way back then, there is no telling where my path would have led without exposing my mind and my surroundings to the intricacies of business.

Aside from the practical and business knowledge he gave to me, my uncle has been a positive and motivating force in my life. Whenever I feel down in the dumps, or I am fearful in any particular situation, I call him, because he is a natural-born problem solver, and he lifts me up every time. He always has a way of making any situation seem fixable. He always draws out the worst-case scenario, immediately eliminating every horrible result that's brewing in my imagination. Before long, my fears disappear, and I forget why I even felt the way I did before calling him.

This is how much a mentor can impact your life. Everything seems easier with them as you have a partner of sorts to walk you through things, and they can help change your perspective. They can motivate or inspire you, which is especially important when things get tough and it is very difficult to continue or navigate on your own.

## *The Wealthy Barmaid's Cousin*

I am lucky enough to have another mentor in my family. He is more of an educational, personal development type of mentor: my cousin. He has always been such a passionate man. He will always be an intellectual, scholar, eternally hungry for knowledge, learning, and bettering himself kind of guy. I believe that his reading list would make the world's most well-read individuals jealous. He was brilliant in school and he was offered many scholarships all over North America for his post-graduate studies. He ended up accepting a scholarship from Schulich School of Business at York University in Toronto for his MBA.

My cousin started working for one the big banks in Canada straight out of college. He was hand-picked by them, and because of his massive potential, they immediately started grooming him for significant advancement. They took interest not only because of his phenomenal work ethic, but also because of the value he adds on a consistent basis.

Since the time I was very young, my cousin always encouraged me to excel in school. He helped me see (as a teenager) that it was cool to be smart, and that it was cool to be well-read on many topics. He always told me, "When we read the works of great thinkers and writers, we are in truth having a conversation with the author themselves." By reading and learning, I could answer so many questions about the world, business, money, and life in general. The more I read, the more knowledge I had on hand to better equip myself for any challenges that I might face. As I continued to read and further my education, everything affirmed his encouragement and perspective.

He always helped me with my projects too, and case studies. He was always there to guide and direct me through education and life choices. He is so inspiring to speak with as well, because he stays so positive, and he is always so full of energy. My cousin is so passionate about everything that he does, and he is extremely enterprising; always on the watch for new opportunities.

He has a "How can I help?" mentality, and I learned so much from him growing up. He taught me the ins and outs of the stock market. He still answers all of my questions, even though he now lives in Hong Kong, and has for the past six years. He is never too busy to coach or advise me, answer my questions, or ultimately just be there for me. I value what he tells me, and I put it into practice. I will forever be grateful that he took the time to be such a positive role model in my life.

He is a great success story in my family, and I am very proud of him. Although he is definitely a capitalist, he is my spiritual, liberal, left-side advisor. He believes in fulfillment in all areas of one's life. He believes in the significance of expanding our horizons in every way, and that this expansion should not be neglected; things like reading, learning new things daily to feed our soul, the importance of traveling, and experiencing new cultures and societies. My cousin consistently works on personal and professional development, which is something we should all condition ourselves to do regularly.

# *The Significance of Tracking Personal Development*

The last component of this chapter is absolutely critical to your success… personal development. I believe your future self is truly the best mentor, as I define a mentor to be a reflection of what you want to become. Personal development should be seen as a life-long journey, and your quest for self-betterment should never end. You should be continuously growing into the person you want to become. You must continuously grow into the person you need to be in order to achieve your goals and dreams. How do we do this?

In order to grow and progress in any area of life, you have to consistently learn new things. You need to have a hunger for knowledge, so you should always read, attend seminars, listen to podcasts, research on the web, and make it a point to speak with others in your field. Any of these activities adds to your overall betterment. Intelligence in learning new skills and information is crucial to your development and growth.

If you are not growing, then you are essentially dying, but once you learn something new, anything at all, your brain will expand with this new information, and it will never go back to what it was before you learned that new thing. In my constant quest to achieve more success, I learned that my own personal experiences were not always enough. Naturally, I started looking elsewhere. My attention turned to books as my primary educator, along with mentors, coaches and consultants. This became my path, and they all seemed to point in the same direction.

You can learn from history as well as the experiences of others. There are success stories that have been adapted into books, and there are coaches who allude to research and proven results. Again, mentors will teach from experience, including lessons from their own consultants. Most mentors work with consultants because they often cite the best practices in any given industry.

There is no need to start from scratch or re-invent the wheel. I learned that you can start where others have left off, and you can learn from their mistakes as equally as you can learn from their victories and successes. It was not long before I realized that I could learn much faster this way. Some of the biggest successes in business and investing are due to this simple concept.

I have learned and applied so much by observing what did and did not work for others in similar industries. This process is called modeling.

You look to the very best people in your field, and then you study what they did and how they did it. You can often repeat their success. You get to learn how they achieved those goals, and also understand the reason behind why they did it that way. Again, it is not rocket science; you just have to be hungry enough for it.

It is important that you actually want to learn, and then you need to apply the knowledge that you gain in order to be successful. If you are looking for alternatives to reading, you can also listen to audio books and programs while you are cleaning up, folding clothes, commuting, or working out, etc. Seek out the areas that will improve your knowledge on any topic that holds your interest.

Any form of education will add to your well-roundedness as an individual. Your potential for success is increased by the combination of your intellectual capacity and your willingness to learn. Learning will always bring progression, building on itself every step of the way, much like a child in school seeing a mathematical formula for the first time. It looks like another language when you have yet to learn how to use it.

Over the course of my life, I learned that it is not important to know everything about a particular topic in order to do something and get started. It is only vital that you know the right things. It is more important to take immediate action and get started than it is to wait around until you have all the answers. It is possible to naturally and progressively learn everything you will need to do anything well, as you move forward. Learning leads to expertise, and continuously learning is monumental to success in any area. Investing is no different, and it is a life-long practice.

Even the most successful real estate investors still learn something new every time they do another deal. Every time that I do a deal, something new happens that I have never heard of before. I just dive in and I figure out all the components of what I am facing; I figure it out as I go, as I'm faced with it. Many in the industry say, "The more you learn, the more you will earn." Learning helps sharpen my judgment, firing my conscience up as a result, and motivates me further. This resulting momentum pushes me to a higher level than I was playing at before acquiring some of this knowledge.

Remember, there is nothing that you cannot do or learn as long as you are willing to apply yourself. Those who take responsibility for all of their choices will win in life. Success comes to those who take action.

# The Wealthy Barmaid Mentors Others

I am a believer that the more mentors and coaches you have, the better. Coaches are best utilized in helping you along the fast track, where you only move forward and rise up along your journey. You do not need to limit yourself to only one mentor/coach – you can look for many. In fact, do yourself a favor by not putting so much pressure on one relationship. If you stick to having one mentor, you could be missing out on different points of view.

Finding a mentor, combined with the concepts of building a network of likeminded, motivated, successful go-getters, is essential for success. In having a network of mentors, you will be able to more effectively create the life, career, and success you want and deserve. Keep in mind if you enjoy watching movies and TV shows on the couch for hours a day: <u>Financial freedom, relationships, and opportunities are not going to come knocking on your door.</u>

You need to get your mind right. You need to hustle every day, because every minute is an opportunity. This comes down to the difference between living a life so tight, always worrying about whether or not you will make it to month's end, versus living the life of your dreams. Take this very seriously and align yourself with these healthy, positive influences that can guide you on your path.

Most importantly, <u>always execute</u>. Take action on everything you talk about, want to do, and say you will do. Much like networking, where you offer guidance and opportunities to your connections in return for what they are giving you, it is important that you mentor others. It is not necessary to be in a formal leadership position, nor will you need years of experience to mentor someone. I believe that each of us has something to give, and I take great joy in mentoring other people. I love it when I can use my own experiences to help others accelerate their growth. I usually reflect on personal mishaps, and I talk people through similar scenarios to help them avoid mistakes that I have made.

It is never too early to become a mentor, and the more you serve others, the more confidence and success will come your way. Similarly, you too will grow in the mentoring of others. As you reflect on the experiences of your life, you will carve it down to the core to better share them with others, and your knowledge becomes wisdom over the course of this. You will never learn something so completely as when you teach it to another person.

# Chapter Highlights

There are two ways to get ahead in life and achieve your goals:

1. Your time, effort, and energy (blood, sweat, and tears).
- Your own trial-and-error method (the slow and expensive way).
2. Find someone who has achieved what you want.
- Pay them for an accelerated education. This is the fastest and cheapest way in the long run.
- A mentor will help you further yourself and your career path to new heights; often, heights that you would never have conceived of before.
- Finding and building relationships with mentors is a key ingredient to success.
- The influence that a mentor can have on your life is priceless.
- There are paid and non-paid mentors/coaches that you can pursue.
- Personal development is critical.
- It should be an ongoing, lifelong journey.
- You need to continuously grow into the person you want to become.

# EPILOGUE
# THE WEALTHY BARMAID:
# IN CLOSING

You are officially on the path to building wealth and financial freedom. Thank you for taking the time to read my book. In doing so, you have invested in yourself and I hope you now feel closer to creating your dream life. Take a moment to give yourself some credit for seeking betterment in both your life as well as your circumstances. Not very many people will do this, and they will not succeed in life, but that is not you. You are already taking action.

It does not stop here. Knowledge without execution is not power. You must apply the principles you learn and continually put them into action. Your continuous action is a necessity for seeing the results and becoming successful, wealthy, and independent.

The timing of your implementation will also be critical as to how fast and how far you will achieve success. I have heard so many people say to me, "I really wish I started sooner. I wish I didn't waste my time debating, thinking, and talking about it. I wish I didn't analyze every single detail to death. I wish I could stop telling myself that I will do it next year or next month when I might be in a better financial position, or when I get a better job." So, to quote our friends at Nike, "JUST DO IT."

They realized they wasted so much time and could have been so much farther along on their journey if only they faced their fears head on, if they just made the leap. Do not waste precious time. Stop acting like you live twice, because now is the time to take action and go after the life you really want. Do not listen to that inner voice of self-doubt in your head, the one that tells you:

- It's not possible.
- I can't do that.
- I can't afford it.
- I'll never be a millionaire.

www.melaniebajrovic.com

Stop thinking small and get comfortable with being uncomfortable, because everything you have ever dreamed of is 100% achievable. At first glance, this book is about building your wealth through real-estate investing, but at its core, it's about making the necessary changes to achieve success in your life. Follow my strategies and not only will you be able to start your journey towards financial freedom through real estate, but more importantly, the skills you acquire will spill over and enrich every part of your life. Success is a mindset, and you now have the tools. Put them into practice and let's make this happen.

The results all stem from your mindset and what you believe, which all follows this methodology:

## *First and Foremost*

- You need to establish what you want.
- This is your goal.
- You need to set clear, step-by-step plans for how you will achieve your goals.
- Set a timeline for achieving each step.
- Hold yourself accountable and make it real.

## *Work on Your Mindset*

- You need to establish daily wealth-building habits.
- Positive habits will compound over time if you steadily progress towards your desired outcome.
- You will find yourself gaining even more momentum by taking consistent action.
- You must overcome your fears and self-doubts, many of which are self-inflicted.

- You must maintain your knowledge of both internal and external obstacles that might stand in your way – ones that may impede your achievements.
- You need to commit yourself to seeing your goal through to the end, cut off all other possibilities, and never give up.
- Perseverance takes you across the finish line.

## Get Your Financial Situation in Order

- You need to rid yourself of any debt.
- You need to set yourself up for automated debt repayment and savings.
- You need to accelerate your savings.
- You need to prepare via budgeting.
- Make sure you are spending less than you make.
- Accumulate the excess funds for investing.

## Invest in Real Estate

- When your mindset and your finances are ready, start investing wisely in real estate.
- Real estate is proven to be the safest, most profitable, and reliable way to build wealth.

## You Do Not Have to Do This Alone

- Keep your eyes open, and start picking out needed help.
- Build networks of successful people.

- Surround yourself with the right kinds of people, mentors, and coaches who help you stay focused and motivated on following through until you achieve your goal.
- They will show you the best strategies to accomplish your desired outcome.

Then put the process on repeat. Follow this process, and watch your network and net worth grow to unbelievable heights. Following these principles will get you to your desired outcome, because your principals and the implementation of them are what set you apart. Not everyone will become financially wealthy, but I truly do believe that anyone can. Building wealth via real estate has always been phenomenal to me, and it has proven to be a big part of my path to financial freedom.

I know that anyone who has it in them to sit down and make a plan will need some ongoing help from someone who is an expert with the process. Because it is not so common for everyone to know an expert in this field, I have created the Melanie Bajrovic Wealth Academy Mastermind Support Group, wealth-building Courses and programs, and mentoring services. I encourage you to reach out and utilize these resources as you progress with your plan.

Aside from this community, another resource available to you is my website, www.melaniebajrovic.com, which I encourage you to use as a tool. There you will find calculators, forms, and contracts available for downloading. And of course, if you have any questions along your journey, or if I can be of any assistance to you, please don't hesitate to reach out. We will do our best to answer your questions and/or point you in the right direction.

Remember, if you do not take any steps today toward your future goals and dreams, you will never progress. If you are not moving forward today, then you will never experience any changes in your life tomorrow…next week, next year, <u>never</u>. As I learned from the wise words of my grandparents:

*If you do not push yourself past the limits of your comfort zone, you will not accomplish anything in life. If you are too comfortable, you will never try hard enough or put in the effort to get out of the mediocrity and familiarity of your current life situation.*

I strongly encourage you to take action in whatever form you can today. I encourage you to commit yourself to making changes. I want you to live your life purposefully, and on your own terms. Life is short, so do not waste it on fear of the unknown, or the fear of putting in the hard work and the extra hours due to uncertainty.

I hope you enjoyed my book and have found the inspiration to take action and make your success happen as soon as possible – for yourself and for your loved ones. Do not allow yourself to be the obstacle that stands between where you are today and where you want to be tomorrow. I believe that anything in life is possible, and my ultimate success is found in helping you achieve your goals. No matter how big or small, your goals and dreams can come true. Mine certainly did.

I wish you all the success on your journey,

Melanie Bajrovic

# APPENDIX 1
## HABIT #5 – DEBT REDUCTION STRATEGIES/GET RID OF DEBT GUIDE

So you can quickly get started investing in real estate and get on the road to building wealth, below is a strategy for getting rid of your debt:

## *1. Track Your Spending*

I like to go old school. By this I mean write all your spending in a notebook: each and every dime. This is a physical reminder, making you much more cognizant of what you are spending your money on by seeing it in black and white, all tallied up each and every day.

List it out with a few columns:

- The date
- How much
- On what

On the other side, keep a running total so you know where you're at with your spending at all times. Or you can go digital as well, using software such as Excel spreadsheets or <u>mint. com</u> to track your spending. I recommend you do this for at least three months to get a really good handle on where all your money is going, and you will fully begin to practice managing your money well. This is a diligent process that requires conditioning.

<u>Do not skip a day of tracking no matter what.</u>

# 2. Make a Budget

Once you know where all your money is going every month, you can start cutting back any unnecessary expenses. If you realize you are spending $100 every week on dining out, it is easy to cut that out because you have identified where it is coming from and where to stop the bleeding.

If you do not know where the spending is happening, then you will not know where or what to cut. Make a budget based solely on where your money is currently going so that it will be easier to direct where you want it to go (into your debt reduction strategy/payments). It will be easier now that you know where it is and how much extra you have to put towards debt reduction/pay-down.

# 3. Time to Get Rid of That Debt!

*Step one*: Make a list of all your debts – every single one. I will explain the snowball method, which Dave Ramsey coined. You will list each debt from the smallest amount owing to the largest amount owing, and you will continuously make minimum payments on all those debts.

*Step two:* Whilst you are making all those minimum payments, you will be working on the snowball strategy; which is to start with your smallest debt owed, and make as large of payments as you possibly can until you completely get rid of it.

*Step three:* Move on to the next debt up from that, putting every extra penny into that debt again until it is completely paid off, moving on and on to the next debt until they are all paid off.

*By rate*: This method above does not take interest rates into account. So another option/method is to again, make a list of all your debts, but this time, arrange them from highest interest rates to lowest interest rates. With this method you start with your highest-interest-rate debt and put every penny into paying that debt down first until it is completely gone.

Then you go down the line and do the same thing one after the other until all debts are fully paid off. Because we are focusing on paying off the highest interest rate debts first, you will not be subjected to paying the high interest rates and fees associated with those debts. These small factors compounded over time make a huge difference.

## 4. Reduce Your Interest Rates

Most of the time today, you cannot call your credit card company or bank and just ask them to lower your rates. You can still try, but do not be surprised if they say no.

Take your highest rate debt, on a credit card for example, and switch it over to a lower-interest credit card, and consolidate any other debt that has a higher interest rate onto that card. It might just be a promotional rate for a set period of time, but it is still better than paying the higher rate during that period. This goes for other debts as well. Switch everything you can to the lowest rate possible.

## 5. Add to Your Income (to pay off your debt faster)

This does not necessarily mean getting another job or a new job, but you could do side jobs. It will not be a huge help but it also will not be a huge time commitment either. If you have gotten or are going to get a raise at your current job, make sure you use that extra income towards paying down your debt. Just continue to live on your current income while committing all extras towards your debt, paying it down until it is completely gone.

Remember that this is only temporary. The pain of cutting back is for the greater purpose of building your future and making it brighter. Sacrifice is the name of the game here, but again, only for a period of time. This process is not forever. You will just need to suck it up through this period if you are serious about building wealth and designing your life with purpose, the way you want it to be, and to end the cycle of living in debt. Otherwise you will continually pay for your past instead of investing in your future.

# APPENDIX 2
## CHAPTER SIX – NETWORKING – ACTION PLAN

1.  Visualize yourself surrounded by extraordinary people

- Start running in the right circles to attract and keep them
- When you are clear about what you want your financial future to look like, it will be clear who you need to surround yourself with, and what you need to do to attract those people
- I want you to be intentional about your professional relationships
- <u>Never settle</u>

2.  Build that network

- Research and write out lists of all the groups, meet-ups, and associations you want to attend
- Mark them in your calendar and start getting out there immediately
- Feel out the ones you enjoy, and make it a habit to continue going to those events weekly, monthly, or whatever their schedules are

- Keep yourself interactive
- Create relationships with key people, and keep in touch with them

3.  Once you have established a relationship

- Reach out to them for a meeting or a call
- By doing this, you will be able to meet a lot of quality people and get the inside track to building a great network
- This process will work for you if you are willing to work the process
- It is simple and it gets you building a network fast
- You cannot achieve your dreams alone
- If you do not try, you will not improve
- Find out which people get it done
- Find out who does what they say they are going to do
- Target the experts
- These people will help make your real estate investments grow, and they will also enrich your life

4.  Maintain and engage that network monthly at the very least

- Your network must grow as your investing and financial wealth grows
- Your network will reflect your net worth
- Take the time and put forth the energy and effort to cultivate these relationships on an ongoing basis
- Again, always strive to give more than you receive

5. Protect your reputation and operate with confidence

- Your reputation is the most important asset you have
- It encompasses honesty, responsibility, cooperation, and hard work
- The habits you build and demonstrate in your career will be sustained for the long haul
- Treat your reputation as the precious asset that it is
- Become the person who people want to be around and want to do business with; for support as well as reputable cooperation

# APPENDIX 3
## NET WORTH STATEMENT

| | Amount ($) |
|---|---|
| **Assets (what you own)** | |
| Real estate (estimated current value) | |
| Cash in bank accounts | |
| Equity investments (business, stocks, bonds) | |
| Insurance | |
| RRSP, RESP, TFSA, retirement accounts | |
| Vehicles (current value) | |
| Personal effects (jewelry, household items, other valuables) | |
| Any other assets | |
| **Total Assets** | |
| | |
| **Liabilities (what you owe)** | |
| Mortgages remaining on properties | |
| Credit card balances | |
| Lines of credit | |
| School loans | |
| Vehicle loans | |
| Other liabilities (money you owe to others, etc.) | |
| **Total Liabilities** | |
| | |
| **Calculate Your Net Worth** | |
| Total Assets - Total Liabilities | |
| | |
| **Your Net Worth** | |

# ACKNOWLEDGEMENTS

A s I sat down to compile a list of people to thank, I realized that so many people played so many roles to get me to this deeply fulfilling moment. I owe a special thanks to those who provided me the life material to write this book and to those who worked with me to write and complete it.

Looking back on my life and those who have contributed along my journey, I see the faces and feel the internal beauty of so many extraordinary individuals. I won't be able to acknowledge them all, but I'd like to start with those close to home - the people who touched my life most deeply.

First and foremost, my family.

My grandparents – who are my eternal source of love, inspiration and unity – there will never be two people like you on this planet. Never will there be two human beings who will dedicate their lives so wholly to their family like you did, and continue to do to this day. The pure abundance of love you've shown me and given me is nothing short of extraordinary, thank you for pouring so much love into me. I can never thank you enough for dedicating yourselves to loving me and teaching me and guiding me so instrumentally in my life. You are a huge factor in who I am today and what I have accomplished in my life so far. Thank you for always being my rock, and my beacon.

My amazing parents, thank you for making it possible for me to have a shot at the life I have today. You have both always been there for me and I know you will always be there to catch me if I ever fall. Your deep love and support you have always given me is very rare and I am unbelievably lucky to call you my parents. Also, I want to thank you for imparting extraordinary standards that have shaped me into the woman I am today. I love you both so much.

My uncle, Dan. Thank you for always taking the time to guide me, to answer my questions, to teach me, to help me, and to shape me into who I am today. I honestly don't know where I would ever be without you.

My aunt Janice. My guardian angel. You were always the one in my corner and had my back no matter what. Your loyalty, commitment, and protective instincts have meant more to me then you could ever comprehend.

My cousins, Julia, Olivia, and Natasha. You girls fuel my life's purpose with your unquestionable and unshakable support of my vision and mission on this planet. Your positive energies and always beautiful smiling faces contribute so much gratifying joy to my existence - thank you! I love you babies.

My sister and brother in-law, I love you. You both gave me the most fulfilling and inspiring gifts on the planet; my niece Leila and my nephew Alen. Leila you are my everything, my angel, my princess and my baby girl. Everything I do is for you. My goal is to inspire you to make all of your dreams come true in this lifetime. Alen, my handsome man, I love you so much and your cheerful yelling and playing loudly with all your heart, throughout the house daily while I wrote this book was my playlist of joy. You are my strong and fearless man. I love you both with all of my heart.

To my nana, thank you for giving me strength by feeding me so well with your unbelievable cooking and for your unconditional love. I love you.

Deepest appreciation to my dear friend Jelena who, for more than 26 years, has always had a unique ability to see things as they really are – not worse than they are – and for always reminding me to be grateful for what we have and what we had to do to get to where we are. My partner in crime, thank you for being there through thick and thin and for dreaming with me all of these years. I could never imagine my life without you.

I want to thank you, Fedza, for sharing ingenious thoughts from your brilliant and philosophical brain and for always pushing me to seek a higher ground in life, and forcing me to see that anything we want to achieve on the planet is possible. We can have it all!

To my coach Trevor, who not only pulled the idea out of me – to write my story, my message and my inspiration on paper and to pursue my vision for helping others (both in this capacity and with regards to my educational programs) – but who also pushed me and reminded me (many times) of who I needed to become in order to reach the next stages of my life and to carry out my life's vision, mission and work - with more energy, joy, and fulfillment. Your unbelievable and always enthusiastic support has gotten me through many difficult times and you have inspired and motivated me more than you will ever know. I am eternally grateful for the role you have played in my development; as a business woman, as an author, and as a game changer.

To Larry at Arbor Books in NYC, thank you for the many conversations, brainstorming sessions and for your guidance in the very early stages of identifying and mapping out my goals and the message I wanted to convey to the world. Thank you for taking my very disorganized thoughts and making sense of it into a readable working manuscript for the first time.

I want to extend my deepest gratitude to Rob Kosberg and the whole team at Best Seller Publishing in California, for bringing my thoughts and words into a finished product. I appreciate you being so patient and accommodating with my several versions, re-writes and edits – and particularly Matt, my editor, for doing so in such a friendly, enthusiastic, and helpful way. Thank you guys so much. The journey was awesome working with your dedication and support of my mission by my side.

Jessica Hume, thank you for recognizing that I had a story and message worth sharing and using it as the subject for your news story to inspire others to take control of their financial situations and their future in a full page article for the Toronto Star – and for the first time (ever) naming me - The Wealthy Barmaid. If it wasn't for that article and the massive response and outreach it received, I would not have started down this path of writing my book and creating programs to help others around the world achieve their wildest dreams; to achieve the life they were meant to live. Thank you!

Carmen Elephante, my dear friend and real estate agent. Thank you for always being there for me, you have been like my second father since the day I met you 10 years ago. I couldn't have done any of this without you. I can never thank you enough for all the time you have taken to speak with me, coach me, guide me, and for being my biggest fan and supporter.

Mark Brunswick my lovingly neurotic and extraordinarily effective and competent marketing and branding director. You have stood by my side as an advisor, a confidant, a friend, a general, and my right hand man. You've always had my back and always have my best interests at heart. You went to war with me on multiple occasions through this journey and my newest venture. These words will never fully describe my gratitude for your existence in my life and what you have done for me. There is no telling where I would be without you and your amazing work and contribution to my dream. Thank you!

Sarah Draper, my brilliant lawyer and dear friend. Thank you not only for your constant support but also for your ingenious work. I feel very lucky to have you on my team.

Beatrice, my trusted and dependable accountant who answers my millions of questions consistently, and who is always keen to take the time to teach me and get me whatever I need in the tightest of deadlines and seemingly impossible timeframes. Bea, thank you for caring, and dealing with such an incessant control freak like me the way you do!

Greg Rollett, my Emmy Award winning digital business coach and trusted advisor. Your amazing mind and your constant innovation in business is inspiring as you help so many people start and grow their businesses. You share valuable wisdom and insight in a way that makes the journey not only successful but also fun and totally worth the ride!

Melissa Chambers, the queen of insurance. Thank you for taking my calls at unreasonable hours and responding to my thousands of texts and emails with answers to my outlandish and sometimes peculiar questions. Thank you for taking the time to help me with my newest venture and for supporting me.

To my videographer and my whole photo team – Ryan Skursky, Adam Ibbotson, Paul Wright, Mella McLaren, Lisa Tuff and Ana Nenoui– who always make me look good on camera and ensure we have some serious fun while we're at it. I can't thank you guys enough for your positive attitudes and the serious quality of your craft. You are the best at what you do and I am grateful to have you as a part of my team.

Last but not least, to my thousands of extended online social media family who follow my posts, articles, tweets, streams, and videos. Thank you for fueling my passions with your enthusiasm, engagement, and your beautiful words of support and kindness. Your comments, shares, and engagement of my mission are like air to me. There are no words strong enough to share my gratitude for you all.

Made in the USA
Lexington, KY
10 September 2017